Democratic Learning

The time has come to challenge many of the age-old assumptions about schools and learning. In this timely book, leading thinkers from around the world offer a different vision of what schools are for. They suggest new ways of thinking about citizenship, lifelong learning and the role of schools in democratic societies. They question many of the tenets of school effectiveness studies that have been so influential in shaping policy, but are essentially backward looking and premised on school structures as we have known them. Each chapter confronts some of the myths of schooling we have cherished for too long and asks us to think again and to do schools differently. Chapters include:

- Democratic learning and school effectiveness
- Learning democracy by sharing power
- Democratic leadership in an age of managerial accountability
- Democratic leadership for school improvement in challenging contexts

This book will be of particular interest to anyone involved in school improvement and effectiveness, including academics and researchers in this field of study. Headteachers and LEA advisers will also find this book a useful resource.

John MacBeath OBE is the Chair of Educational Leadership at the University of Cambridge and Director of the Wallenberg Centre and Leadership for Learning: the Cambridge Network.

Lejf Moos is Associate Professor and Director of the Research Programme on Professional Development and Leadership at the Danish University of Education, Copenhagen. He is also President Elect of the International Congress on School Effectiveness and Improvement (ICSEI).

Democratic Learning
The challenge to school effectiveness

**Edited by John MacBeath
and Lejf Moos**

 **RoutledgeFalmer**
Taylor & Francis Group

LONDON AND NEW YORK

First published 2004 by RoutledgeFalmer
11 New Fetter Lane, London EC4P 4EE

Simultaneously published in the USA and Canada
by RoutledgeFalmer
29 West 35th Street, New York, NY 10001

RoutledgeFalmer is an imprint of the Taylor & Francis Group

Typeset in 10/12pt Sabon by Graphicraft Limited, Hong Kong
Printed and bound in Great Britain by TJ International Ltd,
Padstow, Cornwall

British Library Cataloguing in Publication Data
A catalogue record for this book is available
from the British Library

Library of Congress Cataloging in Publication Data
A catalog record for this book has been requested

ISBN 0-415-32696-6 (pbk)
ISBN 0-415-32695-8 (hbk)

Contents

Contributors

Kai-ming Cheng is Chair Professor of Education and Pro-Vice-Chancellor at the University of Hong Kong, he is also currently Visiting Professor at the Harvard Graduate School of Education.

Mats Ekholm is Director General of the National Agency of Education of Sweden.

Alma Harris is Professor of School Leadership at the Institute of Education, University of Warwick.

Ulrike Löffler-Anzböck is currently teaching German, Psychology, Philosophy, Ethics and Communication at a Viennese grammar school.

Joruun Møller is Associate Professor at the Department of Teacher Education and School Development, University of Oslo, Norway.

Kathryn Riley is Director of the Centre for Educational Management, University of Surrey Roehampton.

Michael Schratz is Professor of Education at the University of Innsbruck and presently Head of Teacher Education and Social Research, Austria.

Per Schultz Jørgensen is currently involved with the international HBSC study as a member of the Danish research group studying health behaviour in school-aged children.

Karen Seashore Louis is Director of the Center for Applied Research and Education Improvement and Professor for Educational Policy and Administration at the University of Minnesota.

Introduction

Lejf Moos

Democratic learning is the big idea running through each chapter of this book. As such it offers a challenge to traditional notions of school effectiveness and improvement, rooted as they are in the hierarchical conventions of schools as we know, and measure, them. The idea for the book emerged in the course of planning for the International Congress for School Effectiveness and Improvement (ICSEI) 2002 conference in Copenhagen. Our starting point was to consider some of the more distinctive aspects of Nordic education and of Nordic society which might lend new insights to the 'movement', allowing participants from the many countries represented to reflect anew on schooling and school learning in their own contexts and in their shared approaches to what makes for good and 'effective' schools. Nordic countries have traditionally represented a very special kind of social democracy and community participation in decisions that affect our lives. In this respect schooling is no exception. Indeed it is central to our concept of democracy.

Denmark, like our Nordic neighbours, has a long-standing tradition of promoting classical democratic notions such as equality of opportunity, freedom of expression and sense of community (as the French phrased it centuries ago: equality, liberty and fraternity). Starting in the second half of the eighteenth century these notions were the source of the vision and the commitment to transform premodern societies into modern, enlightened and democratic ones. These concepts have continued to provide the basis for addressing the many challenges confronting our countries in their development over the next two centuries from agricultural to industrial societies. We believe they are still relevant in our technological age, not simply in the Nordic countries but elsewhere. We have found, in common with people all over the world, that things are moving, that societies are experiencing a process of continuous (and often rapid) change, often in ways that we find hard to comprehend or to keep pace with. One such phenomenon is globalisation: the notion that the world is opening up, that people can move, communicate and collaborate more easily, that goods and finances can travel freely (MacBeath *et al.* 1996).

There are many positive things to be said about this 'revolution' and its impact on the way we live our lives. There are, however, problematic aspects to this as well. Globalisation brings with it fundamental changes, most significantly perhaps in the role and function of national governments. Relations between private enterprise and governments have been transformed by the 60,000 or so transnational companies, requiring governments to negotiate, persuade and convince any firm which decides to move its operations to another country at short notice. No longer can governments prescribe, command or regulate company activity.

In Denmark, in recent years, we have experienced an unexpected consequence of our attempt to open up to this changing world. Fear, insecurity and anger – some of the symptoms of societies in economic and social transition – have given rise to a new xenophobia and a desire to seal off the country and exclude anything that does not fit a neat stereotype of what it means to be 'Danish'. In other parts of the world, September 11 2001 has given a new meaning to the phrase 'a society at risk' (Beck 1986). Instability and the consequent risk to civilisation seem to have become an endemic feature of life everywhere.

For many, the causes of much of this instability are to be found in economic and financial processes. The German philosopher and sociologist, Jürgen Habermas (2001) noted recently that societies engaged in the process of financial globalisation tend to possess four characteristics:

- an anthropological view of human beings as rational instruments willing and able to make informed decisions and to offer their labour freely in the marketplace;
- an image of a post-egalitarian society that tolerates social marginalisation, expulsion and exclusion;
- an image of a democracy where citizens are reduced to consumers in a market society, and where the role of the state is redefined to that of a service agency for clients and consumers;
- a view that policy should be aimed at dismantling state regulation.

These are the building bricks for a neo-liberalist view of the world, says Habermas. The last of his four characteristics would seem to challenge the very basis of democracy. If Habermas is correct (however polemic, and perhaps crude, his depiction) the neo-liberal effort to transform policy-driven societies into market-driven societies is nevertheless accurate. There have to be fundamentally new conditions for democracy, which is composed of three basic elements: the state, the market and the civil society. The civil society is regulated by communication and community, morality and ethics, and trust and reciprocity between subjects. The market is regulated by money, competition and contracts among consumers, while the state is regulated by political power and rules, the social contract and political discussions between (ideally) equal citizens.

The neo-liberal technologies of governance (Peters *et al.* 2000) rely heavily on the market as the basis for, and logic behind, public policy. They are founded on the devolution of management from the state to local level, to local institutions (in the case of education to self-managing schools), to classrooms (classroom management techniques) and to the individual level (self-managing students).

So, governance presupposes agencies of management but also requires, and gains, the cooperation of the subjects involved. According to Foucault (1991) this is the defining characteristic of every modern society. Governance derives its legitimacy not from a legal-rational authority but from the rationale of market efficiency:

> No longer are citizens presumed to be members of a political community, which it is the business of a particular form of governance to express. The old and presumed shared political process of the social contract disappears in favour of a disaggregated and individualized relationship to governance.
>
> (Peters *et al.* 2000: 118)

People are transformed from a notion of autonomous citizens into choosers or consumers of service. So, translated into the school context, parents and their children 'consume' 'educational services' through the exercise of choice. 'Freedom of choice' is the overriding good as opposed to active involvement as members of a community discussing and influencing decisions. This logic – more market less state – then regulates every sphere of life.

In this description we can recognise many of the features of what has come to be known as new public management (NPM). Klausen (2001: 45) describes NPM in these terms:

On a general level:

- decentralisation, privatisation, contracting out
- competition includes public institutions
- from democratic control to market control.

And on an organisational level:

- from process to result/output
- organisations are autocratic and low-trust, in the relationship between 'principals' and 'agents', leaders and those who are led
- emphasis on economic rewards and sanctions
- professional, entrepreneurial leadership
- emphasis on organisations' flexibility.

And we could add to this: 'Educational sectors and institutions are not different from other public sectors and institutions. There is nothing distinctive about education; it can be conceptualized and managed like any other service and institution' (Peters *et al.* 2000: 111).

It seems that the landscape for democracy, and the role of education and schooling in the development of democracy, is being drastically transformed in the following ways:

- What used to be considered welfare societies – those in which the state took responsibility for the well-being of its citizens – are now experiencing rapid privatisation. The state is being redefined as an agency to protect the basic rights of the most disadvantaged, while the rest of us compete for available resources.
- What used to be considered as the citizenry of states – with the civic rights that attend to them – are increasingly recast as consumers. The focus of rights and demands shifts, therefore, from the 'civic' to the 'economic' and 'commercial'.
- What used to be educational institutions, responsible to both national legislation and local stakeholders, are becoming service agencies, answerable to consumers and shareholders.
- What used to be considered as parent-school collaboration is being increasingly recast as a service relationship.

Among the many new demands and changing relationships in education, one particularly important shift has been the stress on efficiency, output and measurement. Educational processes, while clearly integral to educational outcomes, tend to be bypassed and devalued by policy makers who wish to see simple, unambiguous links between intention and result. A focus on values also confuses by introducing uncertainty and debate into what ought to be straightforward and uncontentious. Key ideas and concepts, such as the following, are all contestable:

- output and outcome
- measurement and evaluation
- efficiency and effectiveness
- management and leadership
- consumer and citizen
- restructuring and reculturing
- pupils and children.

Intention and function

It may be argued that the essential functions and practice of the educational system have not changed over the years: a sociological analysis in Denmark concludes that societies expect schools to perform three tasks: they must 'socialise' children, they must 'store' them and they must 'allocate' them.

'Socialising' children means that schools must educate or bring up children in ways that make them fit for the society in which they are going to live: they must be able/competent and willing to enter the workforce, the public sphere, the culture and the private life of the society at hand.

'Storing' children and youth means that schools must be a safe and secure place for children to spend their days before they can be given into the custody of parents or, at a much later stage, into the custody of the labour market. Children and youth cannot be trusted to be on their own.

'Allocating' children means that schools must guide youth into their proper place in the workforce and in society in general. This is typically achieved by testing them in a final exam and on that basis giving them a grade that points them to the way to go from there.

These functions don't seem to have changed much over the years. While the specific form of socialisation varies from one society to another and from one point in history to another, these three basic tasks remain, and are in some respects intensified. Preparing children and youth for life after school has assumed a higher profile. The 'storing' function has been exacerbated by a growing danger in schools' immediate surroundings, while staying on in school, whether at the end of the day, at summer school or for further education, is also on the increase. The third function, 'allocation' has, with a changing job market, also become more of an international imperative, whether in terms of tests and exams as the sifting mechanism or in terms of counselling and 'counselling out'.

As educators we are uncomfortable with discussions framed in terms of functions because they pre-empt the question 'What is education for?' What are its intentions? We find these in the culture of societies, in the mission statements and objectives of the school, in the rhetoric of curricular documents and in the pages of educational theorists who have for centuries concerned themselves with the question of education's essential purpose.

Educational theory in the historical epoch known as 'modernity' (from the late eighteenth century onwards) holds that it is the basic responsibility of every generation to educate the next so that they are able to live in their adopted society. This basic tenet can be found in the work of Rousseau, Kant, Friedrich Schleirmacher, Herbart and others, and is a theme reflected in a more contemporary text, that of Alexander von Oettingen (2001). His argument is as follows:

> Children depend on parents to be educated as they are born imperfect, they are born into a not-yet-condition. They are not able to grow and survive without assistance from the older generation. So, humanity depends on one generation of human beings educating the next generation of human beings.

This upbringing and education includes acquisition of skills and proficiencies, the assimilation and construction of knowledge and the development of motives and values. It is a matter of what is traditionally called 'subject content' and of 'liberal education' – in German: *Bildung* and in Danish *Dannelse*. Children have to learn to become human beings and must therefore be educated so that they are able to function independently in their own culture and in wider society. They cannot go on living with their parents forever but must eventually leave the childhood home and make a living and a family of their own.

Devised in the 'Age of Enlightenment', the vision is one of society as enlightened and democratic, whose citizens are participating and democratically-minded, able and willing to be qualified participants in the community and society. These ideas are still very much alive in the Nordic and Danish discourse. In 1976 the Norwegian philosopher, Jon Hellesnes, formulated an often-quoted differentiation between conditioning and liberal education as two forms of socialisation:

Conditioned-socialization reduces humans to objects for political processes which they do not recognize as political; a conditioned human being is thus more an object for direction and control than a thinking and acting subject.

Liberal education means that people are socialized into the problem-complexes pertaining to the preconditions for what occurs around them and with them. Educational-socialization emancipates humans to be political subjects.[1]

(Hellesnes 1976: 18)

So, continuing to the present day, the ideal of liberal education, *Dannelse/Bildung*, is to educate human beings to be authoritative, competent and autonomous, described in Danish discourse as 'action competent': the individual is able and willing to be a qualified participant in society (Jensen and Schnack 1994). This ideal does, however, rest on a fundamental paradox. It is one that has continued to occupy theorists and practitioners right up to the present day: 'How is it possible – through external influence – to bring human beings to a state where they are not controlled by external influences?' (Nelson 1970 in Oettingen 2001: 9). This perplexing question, addressed by educational theorists a century ago, is still at the heart of the debate about schooling in a democratic society. We presuppose, or know by experience, that children are not able to take care of themselves. They must be educated. Parents educate children, and schools and other institutions educate them on their behalf. Education is, inescapably, an external influence. As such, how is it possible to bring about a truly liberating education? A *Bildung*? An educational socialisation?

With reference to the great educators – Rosseau, Kant, Schleirmacher, Herbart and Benner – Oettingen (2001) suggests two fundamental principles in resolving the paradox: the *Bildsamkeit* of the child and the request for 'self-reflection'. *Bildsamkeit* refers to a fundamental, innate ability to be open-minded and to participate in a shared praxis. The concept acknowledges the child's 'not-yet-condition' – it hasn't yet become what it is going to be – and hence the child must participate in educational interaction in order to become human. 'Self-reflection' means that the self is able to focus its attention on something in the outer world and at the same time on itself. This ability enables the human being to act and to reflect on the action and thereafter initiate other actions. A primary task for teachers is, therefore, to encourage and help children to engage in self-reflection.

Focusing on these principles should facilitate the aim of all educational praxis: to render itself superfluous.

This introduction to the chapters which follow will hopefully serve to frame the discussion of democratic learning and its relationship to school effectiveness. It offers a counsel of caution against a quick fix, a reductionist, managerialist mentality, and reminds us of the essentially contested nature of the issues that each of the contributors were asked to wrestle with. The perennial issue is what kind of citizens a society wants and the consequent nature of the education which takes place in families, in communities and in social institutions. We cannot, therefore, limit our discussions to matters of subject content and curriculum, or to efficiency and effectiveness in their 'delivery'. We must engage in research in, and discussions on, the quality of school life, relations between pupils and teachers, between teachers and school leaders, and in turn their relationship to local and national communities.

In the invitation to the ICSEI 2002 conference we wrote:

> Schools aim to influence the behaviours and cognitions of young people to make them capable citizens in any particular society. It is not only through exposition to the content of school subjects that students find their way to adult life, it is also through the way in which they work during their schooldays. Further, the subject curriculum, teaching methods, teaching and learning are influenced by a multiplicity of cultural, socio-economic and political factors. School improvement and school effectiveness are thus highly contextual issues and discussions on educational reform and change need to reflect any given society's particularities.

Everyone who contributed to, or participated in, the ICSEI conference agreed that democracy was important, but brought to that idea varying interpretations, not only in a theoretical sense but also in a practical sense. In Scandinavian countries democracy is at the heart of education while in other intellectual traditions it is often deeply hidden or, in the worst cases, ignored. There are many reasons for these traditions. For Scandinavians the voices of Rosseau, Kant and Nelson still live in our educational rhetoric while in certain parts of the Anglo-Saxon world the legacy of Locke, Hobbs and Benson, with their focus on rationality and empiricism, continues to exert contemporary influence.

Irrespective of our different intellectual traditions there is a general agreement that the issues touch the lives of every individual in our respective cultures. How we engage in this ongoing conversation between theorists, policy makers and practitioners is the challenge – not simply for the effectiveness and improvement movement, but for all countries who come together with a desire to improve their schools. We do need forums such as ICSEI which allow people to speak to one another and articulate their different educational visions, but we need to constantly challenge the comfortable paradigms and inner dialogue to spark a genuinely democratic debate about where we are and where we see ourselves going in the new millennium.

It was important, therefore for ICSEI's fifteenth annual conference in Copenhagen to hear the voices of school students and parents. After all, how could we discuss democracy in education without listening to their, sometimes uncomfortably challenging, voices?

Students' and parents' voices

Here is a small sample of what students and parents told us. (These extracts have been edited slightly to aid clarity.)

Bjørn Hansen is the chair of the Danish High School Students Association and is 17 years of age:

> I must admit that coming here also made me nervous. It became clear that more than 500 people were attending the conference. But not at all 500 ordinary men and women, no, this was 500 *experts* on education: professors, researchers and leaders.
>
> Now you have to understand, this can make a young man like me very nervous – and the fact that my speech should be in English did not make the problem smaller. But then I started thinking about the theme of the conference. And I came to the conclusion that when discussing school democracy and participation – actually, representing active school students in Denmark, I *am* an expert!
>
> It is not easy to present a holistic vision for democratic school systems in ten minutes. I won't even try. Instead I will concentrate on three important points:
>
> 1 democratic school systems are not only crucial for democratic societies but also for effective learning;
> 2 in order to realise a school system which in reality builds on democratic principles, we must maintain the curiosity, initiative and participation of the pupils from their first years in school; and
> 3 in order to maintain and expand the participation of the pupils, we must from their early childhood involve them in the decision-making process.

A democratic learning process will devote the students to the learning and thus *increase* the learning. Having a say in the choice of topics, materials used and learning process will commit the students to the learning in two senses: first of all the students will choose what is most interesting, which will encourage them to participate more in the process. Second, the participation in the decision-making process will give the students a greater feeling of responsibility for the learning.

So not only is democracy important for democratic societies, it *also* fosters responsible students and thus better learning. The education systems are, even though probably trying the opposite, removing fantasy [from the school and learning] and the will to participate from the pupils. But this does not at all lead me to pessimism concerning the future of real democratic learning. Because in the first graders, in their fantasy and willingness to participate, I see the roots for democratic and effective learning. In my eyes one of the greatest challenges for the development of education systems is to find a way to maintain childish curiosity, fantasy and initiative, and thus participation. This leads me to my third and last point.

I suppose there is a general consensus that pupils and students when graduating should be active, willing to stand up for their views and take a stand in the debate. But what is the first thing we teach the pupils starting in school: to sit down and shut up! Nevertheless, I believe it is possible to build an education system based on continuous progress in the participation of the students, starting from first grade. The culmination of this progression is in my eyes truly democratic schools with democratic leaderships.

But is this idea utopia? I suppose the general opinion is that pupils do not have the responsibility needed for the power they will be given by their participation. Without going deeper into this theme I will share my experience from working with active students. And also from myself having been a pupil in eighth grade not knowing what to say when my teacher wanted me to participate.

My experience is simply that *trust creates responsibility*. Making the students choose a topic, giving the pupils' councils real power only increases the participation and responsibility.

Ditte Maria Molin is a high-school student. She is 17 years old and a Danish representative to The UN Congress on Child's Rights:

According to the UN's definition I'm a child. But I do not feel like a child any more, more a young person. Everyone wants to be taken seriously – even when you are 6 years' old. In all the years you go to school you want to be taken seriously, and the older you get the more you can take a stand – but only if you learn how to. Nowadays lots of students just give up.

In my sister's class, fifth grade, a lot of the children want to be representatives in the school council and the way the teacher figures it out is to draw lots with them. It is the first wrong thing; it is not the right way for learning democracy by drawing lots. The class should have had an election, to make sure that the people can represent the other students.

I asked my sister why she wanted to engage with the school council work, what she knew about it – the answer is scary – she knew nothing. Just one thing. The school council want a soda machine at the school, and hang papers round the school that you can sign if you want, but my sister doesn't. She knows that someone will tear them down anyway. It is one thing to do something; it is another thing to inform. It is very difficult to respect things when you don't know why it is the way it is.

Democracy is a very strange thing, and it is very difficult to set the limit. But the most important thing is to remember us in any kind of decisions, listen to us, and use us as collaborators, not just someone you ask when everything is decided. We don't ask you to turn over all the responsibility to us, but you really have to teach us to make good decisions, teach us to see both sides of a case, teach us to demand our rights – but most important of all – tell us about our rights.

The most important thing of all is to feel like a collaborator, to be taken seriously and to feel the importance of the work you do. I have not done research on this, but I am a pawn in the game every single day, I am here today with an appeal to all of you: if you want to hear our opinion and use us as collaborators – *just ask us!*

Solveig Gaarsmand is the vice president of the Danish Parental Association School and Society and the vice president of the European Parents Association:

In a democratic society every citizen has rights, duties and responsibilities. We have the opinion that we can obtain good results by listening to each other and urge motivation to support the

development of the society through sharing knowledge, information and thoughts. Everybody has a duty to take an active part
in this process. Parents are citizens with a special responsibility
to their children. They have the responsibility to bring up their
children to become good citizens. Therefore they must have an
influence on their children's school. Another reason to give parents influence is the fact that all research shows that parents have
an enormous influence on their children's results in school. As
parents we have a right and an obligation to be involved in the
learning process of our children.

On a national level the first paragraph of the law says that
parents and schools must cooperate and further that all schools
must elect a board consisting of seven parents, who are elected
for four years, two members of the employees (mostly teachers)
and two pupils. They all have the right to vote. The headmaster
and the deputy/assistant attend the meetings of the board but
they don't have the right to vote. The chairman of the board has
to be a parent. The board usually meets once a month.

The Education Act states that the board deals with the aims,
the principles, the development, the curriculum and the budget of
the school. The school board suggests the employment of new
teachers and the head for the school and accepts the annual plan
of activities and the teaching materials. The board most of all has
a strong obligation to make a proper framework for home-school
partnerships in each school.

The informal influence is not by law but by tradition in most
schools. Most classes have one or two yearly meetings with all
parents and two individual meetings with each pupil and their
parent with some of the teachers.

The above mentioned are the formal and informal – to some
extent ritual school-home – relations which are practised in most
schools. An improvement to this is the introduction of 'school
start' meetings for parents when their child begins school. Parents
cannot be expected to know what has changed in school since
they were themselves pupils. They carry with them the notions of
the school as it was more than 20 years ago. Many changes have
been made since. Therefore it is important to open the school to
new parents and inform them and discuss with them what school
is today and why these changes have been made. It is also important for parents and teachers to get to know each other, otherwise
you cannot expect them to be able to be good partners. It is a
starting point for the school to have meetings of teachers and

parents together, offering the opportunity to discuss and get to know each other and to express the expectations each partner has of the other.

It is very important to have equality between teachers and parents at these meetings so the teacher responsible for the class should not be the chair of the meeting. If so you build up a hierarchy instead of a partnership.

Parents and teachers must be partners to give the child as good an opportunity to learn as possible. They are partners in bringing up the child to become a good citizen. Therefore it is important to have a good legal basis of school-parent partnership and to have the will both as a parent and as a teacher and headmaster to cooperate – to the benefit of the child!

Introducing the chapters

Chapter 1 acknowledges the contested nature of democracy and draws on the work of Manuel Castells and his descriptions of 'the new capitalism' – a capitalism of information which serves to widen the gap between the educational haves and have-nots. In this context, school effectiveness and improvement research has to go back to its roots and original purpose, which was concerned with democratic equality. In the 30 years or so of its existence such research has not adequately addressed the tension between this goal and the competing goals of social mobility and social efficiency. The latter aims have been closer to the goals of policy makers and politicians who pursue short-term 'outcomes' (such as those measured by effectiveness researchers) in order to demonstrate links between education and the economy – links that rest more on political pragmatism than on evidence. School effectiveness research, it is argued, has for years been concerned with surrogate learning – that is, accessible measures which can be correlated with other aspects of school functions, not necessarily because they have any intrinsic value. This begs the questions, therefore, of what is learned, how it is learned and how learning crosses the boundaries of school and classroom. John MacBeath challenges the school effectiveness and improvement movement to become more eclectic, less inward-looking, less stuck in its traditional quantitative black box paradigm, to become interested in substantive educational issues, learning and democracy, formal and informal learning, individual and community learning, external and self-evaluation.

In Chapter 2, the question 'How can educators prepare the citizens of tomorrow for the new global and technological revolution?' is posed by Kathryn Riley in the context of contemporary changes and challenges. The basis for looking at societies is the understanding that is both about a broad and diverse cultural range of rich and poor countries and of advantaged and less advantaged social layers. Research and observations of 'effective' and 'good' schools in many different settings reveal a diverse range of attitudes among schools and among teachers, but the 'good' schools seem to be those which are sensitive to local expectations. Different cultural settings offer their own different answers to the big overarching goal – the struggle to build learning communities. Just as that quest is a common feature across countries, so too are the failures of schooling in resolving the big issues: relationships, teaching and learning, time and resources, adapting to change, affecting attitudes and strategic approaches. The question of how to create a social partnership of teachers, researchers, administrators and politicians for future reform is discussed, starting from the perspectives of initiatives in the Third World. The chapter concludes with a framework for tackling these issues.

The purpose of Chapter 3 is 'to render the concept of 'democratic schools' more problematic than resolved'. There is a widespread assumption that democracy is a significant aspect of the culture in which students are educated and it is often assumed in turn that the culture is a strong determinant of student outcomes. On the other hand, schools may be seen as 'mini societies', the basis for the development of democratic citizens. The problem is that the essence of the debate is rarely engaged and the issues remain unresolved. Karen Seashore Louis describes three theories of democracy: liberal democracy, social democracy and democracy as participation. The discussion is illustrated with different types of society and traditional understandings are challenged in the light of recent global transformations. The theories are used as a lens to discuss a number of key questions: what kind of democratic schools do minority groups benefit from? Who owns the schools (parents or teachers, students or government)? What is the relationship between religious schools and government schools? What are the outcomes for children and young people from diverse kinds of democratic schools?

Since the 1920s, Swedish educationists have been inspired by Dewey's Chicago experiments on school democracy with the emphasis on students' participation in schools' democratic procedures. Often, student representatives were elected to participate in committees and boards. In order to find out what effect those efforts would have, Dewey carried out a longitudinal study (in 1969, 1979 and 1994) aimed at describing students' perception of participation in decision making in school life. The results are not encouraging. Only in respect of a few items, such as the school dance and charity collections, that occur once a year, is there evidence (from a student viewpoint) of their increasing level of involvement. In Chapter 4, Mats Ekholm finds in the literature on school effectiveness and improvement a rich and varied body of work but one that isn't disseminated or used in schools, a criticism that may be applied to international and local literature. More fundamentally, his critique of the assumptions that underlie the 'black box' model of schools as we know it underlines the need for teachers and schools to reconceptualise schooling and teaching, and to explore these issues beyond the limiting paradigm of much current effectiveness research: 'As teaching takes place it is sometimes hard for students to learn. This might especially be true for certain topics like democracy learned by experience'.

A starting point for Per Schultz Jørgensen in Chapter 5 is the question: how do children see their own situation in school, among friends and at home? This is fundamentally about democratic learning, power, influence, freedom and rights, in this case the UN Rights of the Child. A core theme is the formation of character, the liberal education that is shaped by the learning environment: 'We cannot expect a mature formation of character in the inner learning environment if we don't allow influence in the outer environment'. Dedicated and democratic teachers, he argues, must try to live up to the new demands of open, complex societies that require individuals to put greater effort into character formation. He draws on the HBSC (Health Behaviour of School Children) investigation', criticising current state school performance in this field and describing a range of initiatives designed to promote student well-being and a competence-based learning environment.

Education is about helping the next generation to come to terms with how things become meaningful within an overall frame, write the authors of Chapter 6. Conventional teaching methods rest on the use of language, words and phrases, which tend to limit understanding because of their familiarity as well as their ambiguity. Researchers too have clung to the linear medium of words to explore and communicate their findings, undervaluing the visual medium. In order to reach the 'inner world' of schools from the children's perspective we need to explore alternative avenues of expression. Michael Schratz and Ulrike Löffler-Anzböck illustrate the use of photo evaluation as a method of exploring the inner life of schools. Photos have the power to 'pull out' from the background of school life and make salient aspects of the learning/teaching environment that might otherwise remain concealed in the background. As their chapter illustrates, students often take photos that depict social relationships within their own communities and shine a new light on their relationships with teachers and school leaders. They bring a new meaning to the concept of 'framing' – the photograph giving a literal 'tight frame' to a taken-for-granted aspect of day-to-day life: the toilets, the corridors, the laboratory cupboard, the untidy staffroom, windows and exits which symbolise escape. These aspects, rarely glimpsed in official prospectuses, programmes and development plans, nevertheless come into their own as significant outcrops in the learning landscape. Photo evaluation, as the authors argue, is one way of giving voice to children and youth in democratising, learning, teaching and decision-making.

While most people agree that democratic leadership is good for schools, they don't agree on what that means, writes Jorunn Møller in Chapter 7. For Dewey, who has been a great inspiration for Norwegian theorists as well as practitioners, democratic leadership meant that democracy was lived through participation in the everyday practice of school life. Current reform initiatives in the Nordic countries as well as in other countries, however, seem to be redefining and reconfiguring the concept of democracy as an economic one rather than a social one. The traditional trust in teachers' work is now challenged. There is more focus on 'power over' and 'power through' models of leadership than on 'power with' models. The emphasis, for liberal reform initiatives, is on managerial accountability, competing with initiatives which lay emphasis on accountability towards a democracy of citizens rather than political administrations. Therefore, the fundamental question of 'Who do we work for?' has to be revisited again and again.

In Chapter 8 Alma Harris outlines the findings from a research study that explored effective leadership in a group of secondary schools in challenging circumstances. The chapter highlights the key characteristics and features of the leadership approaches adopted and argues that the heads in the study operated a shared or distributed model of leadership. The empirical evidence from teachers, senior managers, pupils and headteachers points towards a model of leadership, that is fundamentally concerned with building positive relationships and empowering others to lead. The chapter concludes by suggesting that a fundamental re-conceptualisation of leadership is required, one that equates leadership with the many rather than the few and recognises the fundamental relationship between teacher leadership and school improvement.

In Chapter 9, Kai-ming Cheng takes us from within school to the industrial society at large. The change of societies from industrial to knowledge is, as he illustrates, taking place at a faster rate than the educational system can accommodate. In the workplace the change is from hierarchical to group-based cultures in which human relations are organised in more flexible and less hierarchical ways. In turn, knowledge acquires new forms of creation and dissemination. Traditional, common-sense assumptions of how learning and teaching take place are radically challenged by the type of changes characteristic of the most forward-looking companies. In these we see a greater democratisation of knowledge than is characteristic of educational systems. In a context in which knowledge is produced by individuals, a radical shift in culture and structure must follow, argues the author.

In the concluding chapter we pull together the key points made by the authors of the preceding chapters, for example, differing ways in which democracy is conceived and the diverse challenges it faces. One over-riding challenge across countries represented lies in financial-management approaches to education, which could prove counterproductive to the maintenance and development of democratic citizens and democratic societies.

Globalisation (the theme of the 2000 ICSI Hong Kong conference) underpins each chapter of this book. Each of the perspectives from the contributing authors, representing the UK, the USA, Sweden, Norway, Denmark and Hong Kong, has to be read and judged in the light of this unrelenting social transformation, touching all countries of the world. Democratic learning is a value to which we all hold. Realising it within the demands of a shifting global context and unique national cultures is the challenge we face.

Note

1 Readers should be cautious with the terminology. The translation of Hellesnes into English is based on the Danish concepts of object and 'subject'. A better translation of 'subject' into English would be 'actor'.

References

Beck, U. (1986) *Risikogesellschaft* [*Societies of Risk*]. Frankfurt im Main: Suhrkamp.

Foucault, M. (1991) Governmentality, in G. Burchell, C. Gordon and P. Miller (eds) (1991) *The Foucault Effect: Studies in Governmentality*, pp. 87–104. Hemel Hempstead, UK: Harvester Wheatsheaf.

Habermas, J. (2001) *Warum braucht Europa eine Verfassung?* [Why does Europe need a constitution?]. Lecture given to the University of Hamburg, 26 June, published in *Die Zeit*, 27 (http://www.zeit.de/2001/27/Politik/200127_verfassung_lang.html).

Hellesnes, J. (1976) *Socialisering og Teknokrati* [*Socialization and Technocracy*]. Copenhagen: Gyldendal.

Jensen, B.B. and Schnack, K. (1994) Action competence as an educational challenge, in B.B. Jensen and K. Schnack (eds) *Action and Action Competence*. Copenhagen: Royal Danish School of Educational Studies.

Klausen, K.K. (2001) *Skulle det være noget særligt?* [*Is that Supposed to be Special?*] Copenhagen: Børsen.

MacBeath, J., Moos, L. and Riley, K. (1996) Leadership in a changing world, in K. Leithwood *et al.* (eds) *International Handbook of Educational Leadership and Administration*. Dordrecht: Kluwer.

Peters, M., Marshall, J. and Fitzsimons, P. (2000) Managerialism and educational policy in a global context: Foucault, neoliberalism, and the doctrine of self-management in N.C. Burbules and C.A. Torres (eds) *Globalization and Education: Critical Perspectives*, pp. 109–32. New York: Routledge.

1 Democratic learning and school effectiveness

Are they by any chance related?

John MacBeath

Nearly three decades have passed since the first study of school effects. The impact of the hundreds of studies conducted in those intervening years has been felt at the level of government, local authority, school and classroom. School effectiveness research has fundamentally changed the way we think, introduced a new lexicon of terms and ensured that, for good or ill, schools will never be the same again. But what has that movement contributed to our understanding of democratic learning? It is a highly pertinent question for the future of effectiveness and improvement research. It is time to remind ourselves of what schools are for and what they may become – with a little help from their critical friends.

Democracy – an undisputed good?

Democracy. It is an assumed good although one to which not everyone would subscribe, at least not without a critical testing of the meanings carried within that term (Tooley 2000). Democracy is a value judgement about the way in which a society, or coalition of societies, should be organised, and so before proceeding further it requires a working definition. The following is one among many but is a helpful one in its juxtaposition of individual rights and moral/social reciprocity: 'A democratic society, or a participative democracy . . . is one in which its members are empowered to make decisions and policies concerning themselves and their society but where such decisions are constrained by principles of nonrepression and nondiscrimination' (Pearson 1992: 84). While this is a notion which most teachers, and most people in the school effectiveness movement, would be happy to endorse, a more contested assertion is that democracy is relevant to the nature of institutions and, in particular, to schools. After all, schools can cover a 60-year age range and the whole spectrum of abilities, intelligences and moralities. Teachers, there by choice and profession, bring experience and expertise while children are, it is widely assumed, there to learn from their elders and betters.

Yet, it may argued, without a commitment to democratic processes how well can a school serve the purposes of a democratic society? The two key constituents of Pearson's definition of democracy offer a most relevant litmus test of school culture:

- the personal authority that we allow to children and young people to take decisions that affect them;
- the obligations that we place on them, and ourselves as educators, to respect the rights of others – the moral imperative.

Geert Hofstede's work over a couple of decades has focused on both national and institutional cultures using four dimensions which attest to the democratic, or undemocratic, nature of a society or organisation (Hofstede 1980). These are:

- *power distance*: demand for egalitarianism as against acceptance of the unequal distribution of power;
- *individualism-collectivism*: interdependent roles and obligations to the group as against self-sufficiency;
- *masculinity-femininity*: endorsement of modesty, compromise and cooperative success as against competition and aggressive success;
- *uncertainty avoidance*: tolerating ambiguity as against preferring rules and set procedures.

Against these criteria the Scandinavian countries have performed significantly well and it is to them that we have tended to look as democracy's natural home, their schools being microcosms of their cultures. There is a story, perhaps apocryphal, about the invasion of France by the Danes. When they arrived in Normandy they were asked what they wanted and they replied:

> 'We come from Denmark and we want to conquer France.'
> 'Who is your chief?'
> 'We have no chief. We all have equal authority.'
>
> (Zeldin 1996: 172)

Later they were to set up a community in Iceland, described by Zeldin as 'one of the most astonishing republics ever known, a sort of democracy reconciling the fear of losing their self-respect – which obeying a king would imply – with respect for others' (p. 172).

More recently, in a study of equity (Benadusi 2001), Sweden emerges as one of the very few countries of the world where the gap between the most and least well off has not increased and, if anything, has diminished slightly. Respect for self and others is embodied in the Swedish policy paper *A School for All* (Ministry for Education and Science 2002). The four basic characteristics of the democratic school are defined as:

- relationships and how we treat and value each other;
- the equal value of all people, irrespective of gender and background;
- respect and understanding of differences between people;
- rights and responsibilities in a democratic society.

Realising these values within a school has, however, to be understood not only within the local and national contexts but within the global context in which young people are expected to value democracy and to become world citizens. There is, however, widespread evidence (e.g. Kerr *et al.* 2001) that young people are sceptical of political democracy and disengaged from the political process, an unsurprising finding given a general decline in civic trust among the population at large in most advanced economies (Pharr and Putnam 2000).

Evidence of a widespread erosion of public trust in representative democracy is not hard to seek. In the UK in 1997 the Conservative government left under a cloud of 'sleaze' and corruption, making way for a new Labour government who have perpetuated and even exacerbated the slide in public confidence, reaching a new low in December 2001 with the resignation of the government standards watchdog. In the USA, Pharr and Putnam (2000) have, through successive surveys of public opinion, traced the progressive decline of civic trust. For example, in 1964 under the Johnson administration only 29 per cent of Americans agreed that 'the government is pretty much run by a few big interests looking out for themselves'. By 1984 this figure had risen to 55 per cent and by 1998, to 63 per cent. Countries for which there are equivalent types of data over time (e.g. Sweden and Germany) tell a similar story. At the end of 2001 a right of centre Danish government came to power, riding the momentum of September 11, an event that was proclaimed widely as 'changing the world'. It has, in many significant ways. It has led to a fundamental review of what we understand by democracy. It has recast the debate on multiculturalism. It has had a potentially massive re-educative potential with regard to

Islamic cultures and beliefs and forced us to rethink the interface between religions and politics. It could of itself provide a focus for a whole school curriculum. Writing, with some presence, Castells (1996: 3) noted that:

> Political systems are engulfed in a structural crisis of legitimacy, periodically wrecked by scandals, essentially dependent on media coverage and personalized leadership, and increasingly isolated from the citizenry. Social movements tend to be fragmented, localistic, single-issue orientated, and ephemeral, either retrenched in their inner worlds, or flaring up for just an instant around a media symbol. In such a world of uncontrolled, confusing change people tend to regroup around primary identities.

Teaching about democracy cannot be, therefore, some theoretical or abstract notion. It can only be grasped when we are mindful of its immediate and long-term relevance to children's, young people's, teachers' and parents' experience of the world as they know it. Teaching *for* democracy is a problematic notion in its assumptions about the world 'out there' and the world 'in here', since, for some children, school may be a more democratic place than the society in which they find themselves thereafter, although the obverse may also be true.

For school effectiveness, whether as a research concept, a policy priority or a school goal, such insights are of critical importance. Given that the central measure of a school's success is student achievement, it makes little sense to measure this without an understanding of what achievements mean in their local, national and international contexts. We are all players (or onlookers) in the 'network society' as so brilliantly portrayed by Manuel Castells (1996, 1999). He identifies three key ideas fundamental to our understanding of democracy in and out of school:

- informational capitalism
- social exclusion
- perverse integration

Every country of our world is affected profoundly, economically and socially, by the new capitalism – the worldwide trade in information. Access to information and the ability to discriminate and exploit it for personal benefit is what increasingly separates the knowledge haves from the knowledge have-nots. And year on year the gap widens. This is closely tied to social exclusion. As has been shown (Martin 1997;

Putnam 1999), social exclusion recreates itself from generation to generation and is closely associated with chronic illness, premature death and suicide. Although rates of suicide among older age groups are declining it is rising rapidly among the young. Young people spend more and more time alone, in homes, families, surrogate families or institutions with few supportive social networks. For the less passive and victimised, the route back into the economy is through a shadow economy of borderline legality and criminal activity – a route back which Castells terms 'perverse integration'.

Putnam (1999) claims that Americans, in all age groups, are now 'bowling alone' – his metaphorical index of social capital. Could bowling together be correlated with students' success at school? Could measured student achievement be associated with communities in which there are social networks bringing people together across age groups? David Berliner (2001) argues that there is a direct correlation between student achievement and social capital (defined by inclusive measures such as belonging to formal and informal organisations – churches, associations, unions, clubs – communities of common interest). It is a provocative argument and brings us to the school effectiveness agenda because it is James Coleman that we regard as the originator of both school effects research and the concept of social capital, two inseparably linked concepts.

Democracy, school effectiveness and improvement

The school effectiveness story begins in the reign of the only US president to have been a schoolteacher, and in retrospect one of the most democratic of all American leaders. Lyndon B. Johnson presided over the War on Poverty, the Great Society reforms and, in the first year of his presidency, introduced the Civil Rights Act (1964) against strong resistance. His administration commissioned the Coleman *et al.* (1966) research into equality of opportunity, a landmark study the importance of which cannot be overestimated. Despite much criticism of the methodology, flawed by comparison with many subsequent studies, it was the first time that such data on inequality, on schools and school performance had been collected, data which was to fundamentally change, perhaps forever, the way in which people viewed school education.

The central concern of the Coleman study, and a few years later the Christopher Jencks report (Jencks *et al.* 1972), was with the role of schooling in redistributive equality, and its power to make a difference to the life chances of children. Their concern was with schooling as an educational agency capable of reshuffling the social pack, opening up opportunity to learn and to succeed in and beyond school. It is significant that both the Coleman and Jencks studies were situated in a period in which systematic data collection was in its infancy. Commenting on the data vacuum, Orfield and Eaton (1996: 166) write:

> The United States did not collect such data through most of its history. Poverty was not defined as a basic category in the U.S. data systems until the mid-1960s . . . Officials commonly denied that racial and ethnic data were needed, argued that they would be used for discriminatory purposes and that publishing them would further stigmatise the populations because such data would disclose sharply unequal outcomes. The basic idea was that it would be better off not knowing.

The data vacuum was filled by a radical, and often highly subjective, critique of schooling as an educational agency, as the book titles alone from that era demonstrate: *Compulsory Miseducation* (Goodman 1971), *Death at an Early Age* (Kozol 1968) *School is Dead* (Reimer 1971), *Deschooling Society* (Illich 1971) *The Underachieving School* (Holt 1976) and *Crisis in the Classroom* (Silberman 1973), while in Europe Torsten Husen, Hartman von Hentig and Ian Lister were all penning their own devastating critiques of schooling.

Much of this literature was concerned with what Kozol was later, in 1998, to describe as 'savage inequalities' but the attack was on a broader front, on the nature of the schooling experience, on the very competence of schools to be genuinely 'educational'. Illich was to describe an institution as 'an organisation designed to frustrate its own goals' and to coin the much reiterated maxim that 'school is a gap in your education' (Illich 1971).

The setting for the Coleman and subsequent studies, while focused centrally on equality, has to be understood within the wider current of ideas and socioeconomic movements. Labaree (1997) has recently identified three predominant and competing models of schooling's purpose, each of which (democratic equality, social mobility and social efficiency) has been to the fore in different periods of educational ideology in the USA and which continue to coexist in precarious balance. They are, perhaps, equally relevant to other countries of the world (see Figure 1.1).

- *Democratic equality* conceives of schools as helping to create democratic values through teaching about democracy, developing

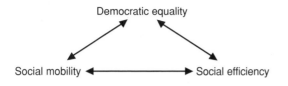

Figure 1.1 Labaree's (1999) competing models

the skills and attitudes of democratic citizenship and treating equality as a valued goal of schooling.

- The *social mobility* goal is seen as offering students, and their parents, a vehicle for acquiring the markers that will give access to better jobs and higher salaries. Wise choice of schools brings competitive advantage which may give the individual that crucial edge 'out there'. School learning is a means to an end rather than an end in itself. This model assumes knowledge to be a private commodity and regulates it through the currency of grades and credentials. Knowledge is measured in performance and performance is necessarily normative – relative to others.
- *Social efficiency* sees schools and higher education as performing a sorting and sifting goal, education's pyramidal structure gradually helping students to find their own level, to continue on, or drop out, as they attain their ceiling of competence or potential. Mechanisms of tracking, streaming, testing and grading all serve to adjust students to a hierarchy of social and economic status with maximum efficiency.

None of these three models should be treated as pure, or even real, but rather as tendencies or emphases. But they do reflect implicit, and often explicit, beliefs about what school is *for*. They are beliefs embedded in political rhetoric and they underpin policy making. Labaree sees the tension among these three models as highlighting the basic contradiction between political equality and social inequality. We might add to this the essential contradiction between democracy in the form of political rhetoric and democracy as it is experienced personally and socially in society and in school. This is not, of course, only true in the USA but in all countries represented within the International Congress for School Effectiveness and Improvement (ICSEI) movement:

> If exchange value is key, then it makes sense to work at acquiring the maximum number of markers for the minimum investment of

time, money and intellectual energy. The payoff for a particular credential is the same no matter how it's acquired, so it is rational behaviour to try to strike a good bargain, to work at gaining a diploma, like a car, at a substantial discount. The effect on education is to emphasise form over content – to promote an educational system that is willing to reward students for formal compliance with modest performance requirements rather than for demonstrating operational mastery of skills deemed politically and socially useful.

(Labaree 1997: 32)

Social efficiency and mobility are conjoined in the reinvention of school failure – another in the sequence of manufactured crises (Berliner and Biddle 1995). These are quintessentially American but are catching and virulent within a global network of political discourse. In the USA, 'crises' date back at least to 1957 and Sputnik, and we have witnessed in the next four decades a succession of attacks on education, on schools and on teachers. A classic text in this genre is *Nation at Risk* (National Commission on Excellence 1983), a highly influential rhetorical document which rested on little evidence and a high degree of unexamined assumptions as to the relationship between schooling and the economy. It posited 'a rising tide of mediocrity that threatens our very future as a nation and a people', a notion that could not be substantiated with any documentary evidence. It went on to claim: 'our once unchallenged pre-eminence in commerce, industry, science and technological innovation is being overtaken by competitors throughout the world' (National Commission on Excellence 1983).

Laying responsibility for this at the door of educators was popular during the Reagan-Thatcher years and has continued under the Blair-Bush axis. Writing on the day of the Programme for International Student Assessment (PISA) publication in December 2001, Gerald Bracey offered an alternative interpretation for the success of American competitors:

Last month, Motorola announced it was eliminating 30,000 jobs in the US and Ireland (previously usually listed among our main competitors). And where is it moving the jobs to? China. For educated workforce reasons? Hardly . . . One would hope that the 'world-wide slowdown' which was catapulted into recession by September 11 would finally wake people up about the lack of school-economy connections. Everyone should go back and read

Peter Applebome's 'Better Schools, Uncertain Results' which noted the lack of connection.

(Bracey 2001)

Twenty years on from the *Nation at Risk* report, newspaper headlines continue to perpetuate the school crisis and the assumed economic link. A December 2001 headline from the Council of Basic Education in Washington described PISA data on America's scholastic performance as evidence of 'a rising tide of mediocrity'. *Plus ça change*!

Against this backdrop, data from school effectiveness studies, increasingly international in focus, can help to demythologise political rhetoric. It can provide counter-evidence of standards and can also offer a more sophisticated understanding of the factors that lie within classrooms, within schools and beyond schools, as against those which lie within communities, within national policies and in the international movement of ideas, policy borrowing, cherry-picking, transplanting and grafting.

Effectiveness – from democratic equality to social efficiency?

The relationship of school effectiveness research to policy development and its impact on school practice is a highly complex and contested one. The movement has been accused of complicity with repressive legislation and held responsible for the direction of current reform (Elliot 1996; Fielding 1997; Slee *et al.* 1998). The sweeping nature of these accusations, as Creemers (2001) points out, fails to take account of the very different relationship of policy and research in different national administrations and the role played by researchers in different countries in supporting, moderating or countering the policy agenda. For example, one of the most influential researchers in the field, Peter Mortimore, has been a consistent and outspoken critic of policy directions under New Labour in the UK, much of that policy emanating from the Department's (DfEE) own School Effectiveness Unit, the director of which was himself a critic of school effectiveness research (SER) (Barber and White 1997).

The three Labaree models provide a useful framework for identifying some of the interconnections of policy and research and unravelling some of the tensions within the school effectiveness movement itself. School effectiveness may legitimately be described as a 'movement' in a number of senses, not least in its progressive development of thinking and in its relationship to both policy and practice. Its origins are solidly in democratic equality. Its starting point is the high correlation between social background factors and school achievement, the single most consistent theme from Coleman onwards. Its leitmotif is school performance and achievement and its implicit commitment is to equity. Its mission is to find a zero correlation between social background and school achievement, the ultimate demonstration of school efficacy.

On the policy front, the school effectiveness movement has moved administrations, often slowly, towards a reporting of value-added instead of 'crude' attainment data. Measures of prior attainment are now more routinely used to measure progress below and above expectation. The movement in ideas and growing sophistication in techniques has been demonstrated in the researchers' more sensitive probing into differential effectiveness, exposing ways in which schooling impacts variously on social and ethnic groups and on boys and girls (Smith and Tomlinson 1989; Levine and Lezotte 1990; Sammons 1995; Thomas *et al.* 2001). Research into gender inequalities in particular has been of major policy significance in a range of countries and a major theme of the recent PISA study.

Much of mainstream effectiveness research, however, may also be viewed in terms of social efficiency and social mobility. Research studies have, indirectly and sometimes directly, furnished policy makers with a formula for greater efficiency. This is truer of some countries than of others and is perhaps most marked in the UK, where value for money, performance tables, standardised testing, value-added and parental choice have been introduced on the back of school effectiveness. The School Effectiveness Unit at the Department for Education and Skills has drawn very heavily on such studies and has employed key people from the movement worldwide to contribute to policy formation and evaluation.

The interrelationship of school measures, testing, performance tables and parental choice, while underpinned by a concern for efficiency, strongly reinforces a social mobility perspective. As Willms (1997) has shown, not only does social mobility drain schools of their most motivated students but it also robs them of their most positive parents. The delicate balance of the social mix is also upset in the process. So the most precious educational resource of the school – its social capital – is depleted. This is social capital as represented by parental expectations and networks and by the high-aspiring and high-achieving students who are a substantive motivational and learning resource for their peers.

We have, in the interest of making our findings accessible (and I personally have to plead guilty) used a language which expresses effects as school X adding one more good pass at A grade as against school Y, carrying the message that school X is a wiser choice for a parent than school Y. If not a measure of intrinsic worth of the school it is, apparently at least, a measure of its extrinsic, or market exchange, value while saying nothing about its value to the learner, to the school community or to society. This shorthand way of expressing school effects has a long pedigree, going back to Rutter, Mortimore and Gray in England, Reynolds in Wales, Wilmms, Paterson and others in Scotland, Meuret and Grisay in France and Belgium, Creemers, Bosker and Scheerens in the Netherlands, Cheng, Pan and Lo in Hong Kong, and Hills, Townsend and Cuttance in Australia. It is, of course, a well-intentioned shorthand for policy makers but its consequences, however unintended, may have been more far-reaching than we would be happy to acknowledge.

School self-management has been eagerly embraced by politicians in many advanced economies for economic rather than educational reasons but, as Townsend (1996) has argued, is unsubstantiated by any evidence that such a policy contributes either to equality or effectiveness. In fact, there is evidence that the further schools enter the commodity market the greater grows the gap between the most and least effective schools and the greater the gap between the credentialised 'haves' and the credentialised 'have-nots' (low credentials serving powerfully to credentialise failure). The greater the deregulation of market forces the more that democratic equality is the loser.

It is useful to bear in mind the Berliner-Biddle (1995: 172) evidence maxim:

- evidence attracts misinterpretation;
- misinterpretation attracts advocates and scoundrels;
- advocates and scoundrels attract the press and the multitudes who prefer to be told tales than to look at the evidence.

While the social mobility model positively encourages parents to opt out of schools and, with growing privatisation, to opt out of the state sector itself, the efficiency model drives schools into increasingly unequal competition. The pressure to raise standardised test scores has led, in the UK, to a targeting of the borderline low achievers, with schools dragging the D-grade students into the benchmark A–C category in order not to be seen as 'failing'. This practice (for which schools can hardly be blamed in a high-stakes political environment), to the detriment of the lowest achievers, is patently in breach of fundamental principles of equality and democracy.

Many schools in other countries find themselves reluctantly complicit in the high-stakes competitive game. It is a trend not restricted to the West or South but impacts on countries of the Asia-Pacific to whom we in the West often look to for a more enlightened approach. When the traditional strong parental support for high achievement is allied to a social mobility view and fuelled by knowledge of differential school performance, it is not surprising if schools and teachers in Hong Kong, Taiwan or Singapore experience a pressure similar to their western counterparts. So, the Confucian view of education (Tang 1996; Lo 1999), having intrinsic value as a public and private good in Asia-Pacific countries, has to be tempered by the pressures of a knowledge economy, impatient policy makers and globalised imperatives.

These policy directions conspire to endorse Labaree's commodity view and the notion of school education as having a high exchange value. To would-be reformers in all countries of the world, Larry Cuban (2001: 7) offers a salutary warning:

> To reformers, teachers are both the problem and solution. Precisely because of this paradox, reformers in every generation have dreamed of a teacher-proof curriculum, texts, and other materials to promote designs that leapfrog the teacher and get students to learn. No classroom reform I have ever studied from reading, through using computers or participated in over the last half-century has ever been fully implemented without teachers understanding the change, receiving help in putting it into practice, and adapting it to fit the particular classroom.

Learning about democracy

School effectiveness has not concerned itself with the 'what' of school learning, nor specifically with what children learn about democracy. Even if this were seen as lying within its remit, data would (in most countries) be hard to come by. The recent introduction of citizenship into the curriculum in the UK does, however, raise some interesting issues for the SER agenda. The citizenship curriculum is premised on learning about democracy as well as learning through the whole range of subjects in which democratic values are promoted. However, in a 1994 study, Whitty found that weakly framed cross-curricular studies such as citizenship do not sit easily alongside strongly framed traditional academic studies. In other words, in order to achieve parity of status in the eyes of young people and their parents, citizenship has to be a 'real subject' and be examined like other 'real subjects'. This would make it possible for researchers to use such qualifications as an indicator of students' acquisition of knowledge about democracy and democratic values and the comparative effectiveness of schools in this respect. Perhaps, in a post-11 September environment, such an initiative would be welcomed by policy makers. A more interesting challenge, though, may be a triangulation of data which probes the congruence, or dissonance, between what is taught, how it is taught and the context in which it is taught.

Teaching about democracy raises a wider question. Is there, or ought there to be, a relationship between effectiveness measures and the content of what is learned? School effectiveness has, by design, concerned itself with surrogate learning. In other words, it has used proxy measures in order to assess the relative, or normative, performance of schools while the nature, quality, texture or political flavour of children's learning has not been within its compass. It can hardly be criticised for leaving fine-grained qualitative study of knowledge and knowledge acquisition to other fields of research but, nonetheless, we cannot deny the power of the subliminal message that has been conveyed about what is worthwhile and what is worth measuring.

In the UK the government's numeracy and literacy strategies, however successful in raising test scores, have resulted in 'collateral damage' (Fullan *et al.* 2001), a narrowing of the curriculum, an impoverishment of the educational experience. This is echoed in Australian early years literacy and numeracy programmes in which 50 per cent of total time allocated to these two subjects, and the other 50 per cent to the other six 'Key Learning Areas'. Townsend (2001) comments: 'This allocation automatically prejudices our views as to what is important, but there has not been any community debate that has been used to justify this'.

A highly effective school may be one which is profoundly undemocratic in the content of the learning while ineffective schools may, at least in theory, engage children in deep learning – teach little but teach it well. Effectiveness researchers have been at pains to give the term 'effective' a neutral meaning and not to confuse it with the word 'good' in any moral or aesthetic sense. They have, however, chosen measures which are often school subjects and generally those assumed to be representative of a core of desirable content – typically language, mathematics and science. Measures of progress in these subject areas are, therefore, taken as a proxy indicator of a school's overall success.

One powerful side-effect of this has been to lend weight to those subjects as 'core' curriculum items. In our own study (MacBeath and Mortimore 2001) we took English language and mathematics as our baseline measure simply because it was too difficult pragmatically, technically and politically to take subjects which lay outside this core. But the decision was taken not without argument and some disquiet and a recognition that we were perpetuating a mythology of what is important in school life and learning. But do these measures, do these subjects, tell us what schools are really about? Has any well known or published study used music, drama, visual art or social science as its proxy measures, or indeed is the notion of the proxy itself where the problem lies?

On the positive side, effectiveness research has made a significant contribution to debate and to uses of data by shifting the focus from inputs to outcomes. It is a paradigm shift that has been widely applauded but it is also a highly problematic notion. An outcome is an end point, a summative measure of what has been achieved. And so measurement of knowledge reproduced on tests and exams is treated as a focal 'outcome' of schooling. This is, unfortunately, an all too accurate term to describe what is, in practice, very often an end point of learning. A large proportion of what is reproduced for the benefit of high-stakes exams is soon left behind. A fraction of what is tested in final exams is subsequently built on and continued into higher education or employment.

Nor does higher education necessarily regard acquisition of school knowledge as valuable in its own right. Examination grades are largely treated as a proxy measure of a student's capability for further study and further exams, very often in totally unrelated fields. When higher education study is in fields that are actually related to school subjects, teaching often proceeds to undo much of what has been learned in school. Employers also treat qualifications as proxy measures, a first line sifting mechanism before going on to select candidates on the grounds of personal and social competencies and the ability to acquire useful knowledge.

Mathematics is an illuminating case in point. The concentration on maths in school effectiveness work and international comparative studies is to a large extent due to the fact that it is easy to measure and travels most easily across contexts and cultures. It is essentially no more than a convenient proxy for comparative purposes and there is nothing in the comparative or effectiveness literature which considers its intrinsic worth or its instrumental usefulness for young people growing up in the third millennium. Third International Math and

Science Study (TIMSS) and Organisation for Economic Cooperation and Development (OECD) data have had the effect of inducing panic among politicians, policy makers and some educators and have served to reinforce the place of mathematics for all, underpinned by the belief that there is a connection between mathematics attainment and economic prosperity. But we need to seriously challenge that most sacred of sacred cows.

When Bramall and White (2000) produced their collection of essays in *Why Learn Maths?* it was met by a media storm, by surprise and outrage that something so deeply embedded in the curricular heart should be so confronted. What jobs do, in fact, require a knowledge of mathematics beyond basic numeracy skills? Less than 5 per cent says Berliner (2001). What kind of mathematics do those jobs require? Not school maths but higher level mathematics, a specialist university study which can be embarked on from scratch at that level, the sum of school maths being acquired by a motivated university student within weeks. What do employers value most and least? asked a Michigan Department of Education survey in 1991. Among the most valued were personal qualities such as integrity, honesty and respect for others. Among the five least valued was mathematics.

While our historic obsession with mathematics for all cannot be laid at the door of effectiveness research it is surely time to begin moving in new directions, exploring new territory in challenging areas such as aesthetics, philosophy (now taught in some primary schools), performing and visual arts, sport, and civics and citizenship – the latter offering one potential forum for learning about democracy. Indeed, many in the effectiveness field are taking an increased interest in 'new learning' (Creemers 2001; Townsend 2001; Stoll *et al.* forthcoming) and its relationship to teaching and school effectiveness. Devising measures of 'learning how to learn' is the focus of a three-year Economic and Social Research Council (ESRC) project currently being carried out by a research team from Cambridge and Reading Universities, the Open University and King's College London. Learning to Learn is one (as yet empty) of the indicators being worked on by the European Commission (2000).

Norway's curriculum framework, with its humanistic conception of what knowledge is of most worth, presents an intriguing challenge to measures of effectiveness. Its seven areas deemed worthy of study are:

- the spiritual human being
- the creative human being

- the working human being
- the liberally educated human being
- the social human being
- the environmentally aware human being
- the integrated human being.

Taken together these provide a comprehensive framework for democratic learning and a challenge to the SER agenda. The task for this decade is to begin to build the bridges with learning and curriculum theory, ethnographic and sociological studies of schooling, education out of school and lifelong learning. Cheng (2001), defines 'a third wave paradigm' of effectiveness which he calls 'interface effectiveness'. It is concerned first and foremost with self-learning, with maximising multiple intelligences, with the IT environment and with the sustaining of lifelong learning. Creemers (2001), reviewing past issues of the *School Effectiveness and Improvement Journal*, finds no evidence of IT as a relevant theme, a telling omission from the literature. A wide-ranging survey of expert opinion on the SER literature by Teddlie *et al.* (2000) reported some significant gaps, in particular those lying closest to the day-to-day concerns of teachers. They conclude that we have given too much attention to measuring the 'vessel' of schooling and too little to the content of that vessel.

The critique is applied as much to school improvement as to effectiveness. School improvement has been primarily about increasing effectiveness at a whole-school level as exemplified in the work of John Gray and his colleagues (1999) who found three forms of improvement which they termed the tactical, the strategic and capacity building. The tactical form is very specifically outcome focused. It is about raising levels of measured attainment and demonstrating an improvement in results year on year. A broader goal takes a more strategic and longer-term focus on achievement and recognises that pushing up test scores is a short-term and ultimately self-defeating approach. The third form – capacity building – is about developing organisational resilience and flexibility to meet and lead change. It rests on an act of faith, or conviction, that one of the outcomes of such a policy will be demonstrably raised pupil achievement. It could be argued that the real outcome is the built capacity of the school, an organisation which will serve future generations of pupils not just this current measured cohort. We might also describe as a powerful outcome the learning of teachers – the ultimate gatekeepers of change for generations of young people to come as well as a high quality professional resource for generations of teachers in the future.

By any of the three Gray *et al.* definitions of improvement the content of what children are learning is not immediately relevant. Not really our business then as school improvers? Perhaps not. It may, though, prove increasingly difficult in our work as consultants and critical friends to bypass the 'what' of learning when offering support to school management in clarifying priorities or in improvement planning. It is legitimate to ask whether improvement ought to be about the substance of what children learn rather than simply the form. Is knowledge of democracy, the challenge to western notions of democracy, the terrorist threat to those democracies, relevant to the teacher of mathematics as well as history? Is there a connection between *what* children learn and *how* they learn, and how they themselves build capacity and deal with change?

There are some in the school improvement camp who believe that capacity building is as much about student empowerment as about the professional development of teachers, and that living and acting within a democracy – writ small – is inseparable from learning about democracy – writ large. Ongoing ground-breaking work on pupil voice by people who would regard themselves as school improvers (Fielding and Bragg 2003; MacBeath *et al.* 2003) does take a closer interest in the relationship of the how and the what of learning, working on those themes in alliance with others from a sociological tradition (Arnot Reay 2001).

Many of us working in this field are teachers and educators, some with a background in equal opportunities, multicultural and anti-racist education, gender research, environmental and development education. Some are veterans of the age of dissent, nurtured on *Teaching as a Subversive Activity* (Postman and Weingartner 1970), seeing the central mission of schools as confronting a world that is becoming progressively less democratic and moving progressively away from, rather than towards, the values which we as educators hold to be self-evident.

It is hard to justify a crisp demarcation between school improvement and what we know from a rich body of research on the quality of children's lives in and out of school. The more we learn of the interconnectedness of feeling, motivation, engagement and knowledge acquisition, the less easy it is to abstract content from the improvement equation. The more we explore notions of knowledge creation and transfer, the more difficult it becomes to draw discrete boundaries around 'school' improvement. The more we understand about the complexity of school and classroom life, the less easy is the separation between the content, the process and the context in which learning takes place. That is why we must also test school effectiveness against the idea of learning in a democracy.

Learning in a democracy

School effectiveness research has made a significant contribution to putting inequalities of attainment by gender, ethnicity and social class on the policy agenda. If we intuitively knew that schools were different for different children we now have more accurate insights into why and how that should be so. French and Belgian researchers (Grisay 1999; Demeuse *et al.* 2001; Meuret 2001), with their focus on equity and inequity, have demonstrated both at country and school level the disparities which separate the most from the least privileged and just how undemocratic schools and school systems can be. Confirmation of this is provided again by the PISA data which compare the distance between the highest achieving and lowest achieving and compare three high performing countries – Finland, Korea and the UK. By far the highest disparity between the attainment of the top and bottom 10 per cent is in the UK.

While the UK celebrated its elevated position in the global league tables, from a democratic equality point of view the more hidden message was a disturbing one. Measures of variance within schools have been used less as an indicator of effectiveness within SER, which has tended to rely more heavily on the mean. Nor have SER studies concerned themselves with the experience of being 'different', or with the inner workings of democratic equality. Researchers have not confronted schools' inability or unwillingness to create a tuned-in, intelligent, responsive anti-discrimination culture.

While effectiveness research has consistently cited home-school relationships as one of its key indicative factors we have had to turn to other sources to learn about what it means to cross that bridge for children of different backgrounds. While this is not, of course, the core business of SER, we will, nevertheless, have to make greater efforts to bring together quantitative school and classroom level data with the ethnographic studies of children's and young people's experience of schooling.

There is a rich seam of literature which both complements and confronts SER studies. For example, in their book *Construction Sites* Ward and others (Ward 2000) document the experiences of Afro-American girls in the USA and the failure of schools to address or to understand issues of identity, self-esteem and achievement. Ward describes how Marie's mother teaches her to survive in a racist society and school system. She teaches her children specific skills, including how to take a critical perspective, the ability to detect racial stereotypes and the capacity to understand how images shape perceptions and often distort the truth. Most importantly, Marie's mother instils in her daughter a desire to resist either emulating or internalising the media images and stereotypical characterisations of Afro-American people, their values and cultural beliefs. But is this not what schools aim to teach? Yet, these accounts consistently suggest that lessons learned in the family fail to connect with what is learned in school. The evidence is that the academic self-esteem of black girls declines cumulatively through school.

There are parallels in the experience of white girls according to Bem (1983), who describes how mothers help their daughters cope with gender socialisation and inequalities. And boys too have their own struggles to overcome, as one Jewish boy says: 'You've got to leave some things at home to make it here. If you come to this school and bring the baggage of your home background, you'll likely meet with more failure than success' (p. 266). Leaving the baggage of one's home background behind is critical to our understanding as researchers. Home background is a vital independent variable. Parental involvement and home-school relationships emerge consistently as factors of effectiveness, but what does this mean and, most importantly, what does it mean for school improvement? How can schools transcend the rhetoric of 'partnership' and 'involvement'?

It seems that in school effectiveness and improvement we have barely scratched the surface of that critical interface. We have manifestly failed to explain what it is that helps children to make sense of the various worlds they inhabit and what it is that schools and teachers do to address that most critical of all issues in educational improvement. This is the subject of Judith Harris' (1998) devastating critique of the nurture assumption and the central thesis of Martin Thrupp's (1999) plea to effectiveness researchers to 'get realistic' about the power of the social mix. Strong endorsement for its importance is a theme of the PISA study which claims that its effects are greater than any other measure, including prior attainment.

This is not new territory for effectiveness research as the compositional effect has been well documented (Willms 1985; Sammons 1995; MacBeath and Mortimore 2001), but we do lack qualitative data on how it works and what its impact is on young people, their motivation, achievement and engagement with school learning. French studies of children from multilingual backgrounds (see maternelle.com) reveal that even at the age of 5 or 6 children hide their capabilities from their peers so as not to appear different and that teachers' ignorance of these hidden social factors leads them to assume individual learning difficulties. This is the phenomenon described by Judith Harris (1998) as the 'Cinderella syndrome'. She describes how children and young people inhabit the different worlds of classroom, home and peer group and indeed become different people in different contexts – engaged and disengaged, drudges and princesses, frogs and princes. Which one of these multiple personalities are we able to capture in our baseline measures? How successful have we been, or might we be, in identifying what effective schools do to bridge these various environments of learning? What do effective schools do to engage young people across the boundaries of age, ability, class, gender and ethnicity?

There is scant evidence of schools as democratic communities meeting the definition proposed by Pearson (see p. 19). The most well-known globally is A.S. Neill's Summerhill School in England. Fifty years on, Summerhill is still following Neill's principles under the leadership of his daughter, Zoe Readhead.

The well-known centrepiece of Summerhill's democratic government is its twice weekly community meeting, chaired by one of the students, at which teachers, cooks, ground staff and students all have an equal voice and one vote. This is a most impressive occasion in its genuine respect for the youngest and most dissident voice and its willingness to open up the most contentious views in public.

Summerhill's cardinal principle of allowing children to decide for themselves whether or not to attend classes brought it into head-on confrontation with the Department for Education and Employment (DfES) and the Office for Standards in Education (Ofsted). In September 2000 in the Royal Courts of Justice the school robustly defended its right to stick to its founder's principles. The government side, anticipating an embarrassing climb-down, abandoned its demands in what amounted to a virtually complete concession. When the proposition was offered to Zoe Readhead, however, she said she could not accept. It would have to be put to the whole school community for a decision. At this point the court was cleared, the three places on the tribunal bench were taken by three Summerhill students and the whole school debated for one hour whether or not to accept the Secretary of State's offer. They eventually did with their own caveats. It was not simply a signal historic victory but a powerful lesson for Summerhill students in the workings of democracy.

At the heart of this court case was the effectiveness question. Is effectiveness to be judged by how well a school meets its own aims and values or by a standardised (some might say 'political') definition of 'effectiveness'? Summerhill students' examination grades compared unfavourably to norms in state schools. While Summerhill's counsel argued the case on the former grounds the prosecuting government department argued their case on the latter grounds. Without the benefit of value-added data it was difficult to make judgements about the school's relative performance but it would hardly be surprising if Summerhill failed to meet the standard criteria of an effective school. Many of the young people attending Summerhill expressed in strong terms how stifled and frustrated they felt by the 'effective' schools they had attended previously. It put into sharp focus the question of 'effectiveness for what?'

It is, of course, not a matter of either effectiveness or democracy. Summerhill could be more effective in the conventional sense of that term but, as they illustrate at the extreme, learning in a democracy will always be about making choices, informed and sometimes not well informed, taking risks and learning from mistakes.

In his provocatively entitled book *Scared of the Kids?* (2001) Stuart Waiton poses that question in the context of Scottish communities which imposed a curfew on young people in the evenings, requiring them to be in the house by 9 p.m. Posing that question in a school context confronts the apparent passion for control, rules and conformity. It may explain the failure of schools to challenge the orthodoxy, to prefer the self-silenced to the resisters, the rule observers to the rule breakers and the conformists to the subversives, although it is from the ranks of the latter that may be recruited the most creative and successful of entrepreneurs and social reformers.

Schools must become more sensitive to the way in which they 'do' differences, concludes Reichert (2000: 270). He documents boys expressing regret at the compromises they had to make throughout their school lives, writing many years later with regret and even bitterness at schools' failure to confront injustice and inequality and even worse to actually (subtly or overtly) reinforce it.

The role of the school as a democracy, confronting injustice and inhumanity, is simply expressed in Hartmut von Hentig's (2001) book of letters to Tobias, his nephew. The book is a series of answers to the question 'Why should I go to school?' In one of his letters entitled 'A school is a city in miniature' (p. 47) Hentig writes:

> Do you really know why Norwegian people don't want to join the European Union? Why there are young Nazis in our country? Do you have opinions about the necessity or danger of genetic

engineering? What a good school is? I have no desire to live next to people who don't have this kind of education. It would be too dangerous. They could too easily choose another Hitler. They could endanger our very democracy. In school we learn to test carefully what is true, for example, this very letter that I am writing to you.

The letters are all about what it means to live in a democratic school in which even the values being advocated by learned and well-meaning uncles have to be tested. There are resonances in this with Postman and Weingartner's (1970) advocacy of crap detecting. There is in this and the following passage a parallel with John Dewey's alliance of what is taught and the milieu in which its taught – scientific inquiry and the democratic classroom and school in which lessons of life are learned both implicitly and explicitly:

> In school you meet people different from yourself from different backgrounds, children you can observe, talk to, ask questions, for example someone from Turkey or Vietnam, a devout Catholic or an out and out atheist, boys and girls, a mathematical whiz kid, a child in a wheelchair . . . I believe whole heartedly that the open school is there first and foremost to bring young people together and to help them to learn to live in a way that our political society so badly needs.
>
> (Hentig 2001: 47)

As Levin (1999) argues, this should not be viewed as a matter of choice, to be or not to be democratic, because the process of education is by definition a democratic process. You have to do it for yourself. It can't be done to you or for you: 'Schooling is organized to have things done to students according to someone else's plan of what will produce the desired results. Such a view is incompatible with notions of democracy, and also incompatible with the concept of education' (Levin 1998: 6). Learning in a democracy, argues Levin, is not *for* anything, for some ulterior goal, for the economy, for employment, for democracy 'out there'. It is an end itself. You have to do it with others because it is a social activity and it is about learning to make decisions and take risks because the greatest disservice that schools do is always to be right, implanting a belief that learning and experimentation is about getting the *right* answers.

There are, of course, many examples of teachers working diligently to educate in a democracy, to listen carefully to their pupils' voice, to create a critical and moral discourse within their classrooms, to expose inequality and challenge inequity, to model by their own actions a democratic way of being. These are people that can be valuable allies in school improvement, when that private practice becomes multiplied and energises others.

Learning democratically

> The school of the 21st century should be a school centred around children and young people. Their influence over their own situation at school must therefore be extended and improved. Pupil democracy and involvement must be regarded as part of the learning situation. Pupils' viewpoints, opinions and wishes together with their needs and experiences must form the basis of the planning of the entire school's activities.
>
> (Ministry of Education and Science 2002)

There is a thin dividing line between learning in a democracy and learning democratically. It is, however, important to stress the latter because when we focus on the learning process as well as the conditions of school and classroom context we get closer to the heart of what school ought to be about:

> If the overall problem of the system is student performance on higher order cognitive tasks this problem will be present in very different forms in every classroom where it occurs. Different groups of students will have different prior knowledge of the basic concepts and different attitudes toward the importance of knowing them. Different groups of students will bring different cultural, linguistic and cognitive understandings to bear on the problem. At the school level, differences at the classroom level aggregate into the overall cluster of expectations for learning, order and engagement into the structure of opportunities that determine whether students get access to the content and teaching at all, and whether they get it in a form that engages them.
>
> (Elmore 2000: 12–13)

Learning democratically means that within highly diverse groups, more and less privileged, more and less ready to engage, all pupils have an entitlement to the best available knowledge on learning effectiveness – how learning happens and how schools provide for that to happen. Rather than taking learning and teaching for granted, students and teachers need to explore together the deeper mysteries of knowledge acquisition, confronting questions such as:

- What is learning?
- What happens when you learn something?
- How do you know when you have learned something?
- Why do we forget things?
- How can we learn to remember things better?
- Where do I learn best? How and with whom?

Yet, argues Elmore (2000: 20) the problem lies deeper:

> The existing institutional structure of public education does one thing very well. It creates a normative environment that values idiosyncratic, isolated and individualistic learning at the expense of collective learning. This phenomenon holds at all levels: individual teachers invent their own practice in isolated classrooms, small knots of like minded practitioners operate in isolation from their colleagues within a given school, or schools operate as enclaves of practice in isolation from other schools. In none of these instances is there any expectation that individuals or groups are obliged to pursue knowledge as both an individual and a collective good . . . Privacy of practice produces isolation. Isolation is the enemy of improvement.

When teachers are deprived of opportunities (or motivation) to learn it sets the model and conditions for pupil learning – seen by and large as an individual acquisition rather than a collective one, seen as learning which must be reproduced in examination conditions where cheating is the most venal of sins.

It is said that 10,000 or more pages are added to worldwide web every hour. The web is in many senses a democratic medium, an abundance of information (and misinformation) for the asking. It is but one source, and probably less influential than the information (and misinformation) that passes from pupil to pupil. It is calculated that we spend about 3 per cent of our lives in school (unless we are teachers) but anything up to half of that time may be in informal knowledge and attitude exchange among peers. There is a naivety about curriculum developers who use language such as 'delivery' and assume a high degree of correspondence between what the curriculum intends and what children learn. Informal knowledge exchange in and out of school is fundamentally democratic but often dissonant with the formal knowledge transmission from teacher to pupil, implicit in Elmore's critique.

School effectiveness has explored teacher effectiveness, processes of instruction and instructional leadership, and improvement has taken as a significant focus teacher learning, but both these streams of research have paid less attention to the ways in which pupils learn or to the process by which teacher and pupil learning mirror one another. Exploring this relationship is critical because the more pupils take responsibility for their own learning the less becomes their dependence on teachers. For example, self-assessment has been shown to have great potential for raising performance with children as young as 5 (Black and Wiliam 1998) because the crucial success factor was dialogue with pupils about what they were aiming to achieve. In consequence, pupils became more committed and effective learners, learning to reflect on their own achievements and thereby improve them.

Nor have we, at least until recently, given enough emphasis to pupil voice. The collection of pupil views through questionnaire and interview has become a stock in trade of effectiveness studies but primarily as a data source. Susan Groundwater-Smith (1999) argues for moving beyond this limited view of students and towards a more collaborative practice in which students become active change agents in their 'own lifeworld conditions'.

In one of the schools in our ESRC study (MacBeath *et al.* 2001) the headteacher, also the class teacher, described her own journey with her class through six stages:

- *Stage 1*: delivering the curriculum. Fitting with the traditional role of the teacher as passing on curricular content from one who knows to those who don't.
- *Stage 2*: beginning to discuss with pupils the purposes and objectives of what they are learning. What is the objective of your learning?
- *Stage 3*: involving pupils in considering and writing down indicators by which to measure their achievement. How will you know when you have learned something?
- *Stage 4*: involving pupils in assessing their own and others' work. How good is this piece of work? What criteria can be used to judge it?
- *Stage 5*: pupils become determiners of learning. They make decisions about the when, how and what of classroom learning. What is the best way to do this?

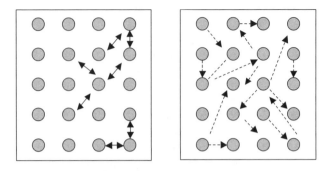

Figure 1.2 Social bonding and bridging – two classroom scenarios

- *Stage* 6: collaborating with pupils as learning partners. What shall we do together to improve the conditions, processes and evaluation of our learning?

There is a parallel here with Otero *et al.*'s work (2000) which posits a move from isolated learners, through engaged learners to introspective and interactive learners, then finally to 'global self-regulated learners'. This can only be accomplished by a radically changed teacher-learner relationship, not only at classroom level but at whole-school level – a challenging agenda for school improvement and the work of critical friends (Swaffield 2002).

The process exemplified by the headteacher as listed above resonates with theories of social capital, writ small. At classroom level we can see the three key concepts of social bonding, social bridging and vertical as against horizontal linking. In Stage 1 the classroom resembled that represented by the diagram on the left of Figure 1.2 – some strong social bonds among a few friends who liked to work together because they were good pals, but leaving some other individuals isolated. The vertical link to knowledge was through the teacher on whom the class depended for delivery. By Stage 5 the classroom could be described more in terms of social bridging, with many but weak links. That is, pupils had been weaned away from friendship bonds to using others in the class as resources for particular skills and episodes of learning.

The more embedded this becomes in 'the way we do things round here' the less easy it is to separate out individual competencies and intelligences, because these are distributed:

Social capital flows from the endowment of mutually respecting and trusting relationships which enable a group to pursue its shared goals more effectively than would otherwise be possible . . . It can never be reduced to the mere possession or attribute of an individual. It results from the communicative capacity of a group.

(Szreter 2001: 3)

Effectively improving schools are most likely to be those which enjoy communicative capacity (Gray *et al.* 1999). The principles of social bonding and bridging, vertical and horizontal linking, are also relevant at whole-school level. The improvement literature has put us on familiar terms with social bonding (Stoll and Fink 1996; MacBeath and Stoll 2001), particularly in secondary schools where teachers cluster in friendship groups or subject departments, the classic 'balkanisation' which is inimical to an improvement culture. When there is social bridging – teachers working democratically, horizontally, to share practice, observe and learn from one another – there is a much greater chance of teacher-led school improvement, so powerfully exemplified in the work of David Frost and his colleagues (2000).

It is not easy to see how school improvement can address one facet of learning democratically without addressing the other. Can teachers learn collegially and democratically without this being mirrored in their pupils' learning? Can pupils build social capital within their own classrooms without it being embedded in school culture and structure? This presupposes an approach to school self-evaluation which goes beyond the performativity agenda (Watkins 2001), which is not simply an inner replication of the inspectorate process but which explores what learning means in its multiple manifestations and contexts. It requires an approach which juxtaposes the differing understandings, expectations and priorities of different stakeholder groups (Moos and MacBeath 2001). Citing the work of Schratz (1997), Alvik (1996) and MacBeath (1999) on school self-evaluation, Lesley Saunders (2000: 423) writes:

Now if liberal democracy means, among other things, accepting that the social debate is one of constant negotiation between unresolvably competing standpoints (Grayling, 1997), it calls into question one of the tenets of school effectiveness, namely, the overriding need for unity of purpose and vision. What about the muttering minority who do not agree with, and therefore cannot be committed nor contribute to, the consensus view? Are they

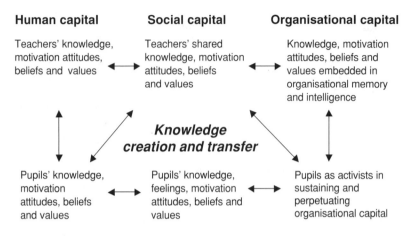

Human capital

Teachers' knowledge, motivation attitudes, beliefs and values

Social capital

Teachers' shared knowledge, motivation attitudes, beliefs and values

Organisational capital

Knowledge, motivation attitudes, beliefs and values embedded in organisational memory and intelligence

Knowledge creation and transfer

Pupils' knowledge, motivation attitudes, beliefs and values

Pupils' knowledge, feelings, motivation attitudes, beliefs and values

Pupils as activists in sustaining and perpetuating organisational capital

Figure 1.3 Linking the human, social and organisational capital

to be castigated and sidelined? Or accepted and possibly even welcomed for their capacity to shed a different sort of light?

Saunders describes the English model as 'instrumentalist, action-oriented, rationalistic and managerial', failing to reflect the fact that different stakeholders experience school differently, think differently, learn differently and have different priorities. Their involvement, she writes, 'in evaluation decisions, processes and instruments is a good indicator of democracy in practice' (p. 424).

Figure 1.3 is an attempt to depict the interrelation of teacher and pupil knowledge creation and transfer and to link the human, social and organisational capital. It may be seen as beginning to sketch an outline and agenda for school self-evaluation and for future school effectiveness and improvement inquiry.

Beyond the school effect

The preceding discussion is, of course, set within the parameters of the 'black box' school. It takes for granted many of the deeply embedded conventions and assumptions of schools as we have known them. It relies for its statistical analysis on age-related curricula and testing, on classes and class teachers, on layers and hierarchies of responsibility and function, and on some crisp separation of the school from its communities. Without this the 'school effect' is impossible to hunt down and value-added becomes an elusive equation.

Comparative country data and national value-added tables are already of dubious validity given the value-added outside school in *jukus* (cramming schools) in Japan, private tuition and supplementary schools. As Sung-Sik Kim (2002) has demonstrated in the Korean context, Korea's pre-eminent place in the PISA ranking owes much to private extracurricular coaching, not to the quality of what goes on in classrooms. Given the slow but accelerating tendency for home schooling and de-schooled learning, the radical shift in paradigm for the future will be from school effectiveness to learning effectiveness.

In summary

School effectiveness has radically shifted the ground on which the debate about school takes place. It has deeply affected policy in countries around the world, sometimes directly and sometimes more indirectly. It has been the object of critique from many quarters, sometimes defensive in reaction, but also showing evidence of how we have learned and moved on, both in sophistication of technique as well as in the compass of the field. Democratic learning presents a further challenge because it goes to the heart of what school is for, what learning is for, and asks us to revisit what effectiveness and improvement are for and what that means in a changing world context.

References

Alvik, T. (1996) *School Self-evaluation: A Whole School Approach*. Dundee, UK: CIDREE.

Arnott, M. and Reay, D. (2001) How pupils can help teachers improve the social conditions of learning. Paper delivered at the American Educational Research Association, Seattle, 18 April.

Barber, M. and White, J. (1997) *Perspectives on School Effectiveness and School Improvement*. London: Institute of Education.

Bem, S.L. (1983) Gender schema theory and its implications for child development: raising gender-schematic children in a gender-schematic society, *Signs*, 8: 598–616.

Benadusi, L. (2001) Equity and education: a cultural review of sociological research and thought, in W. Hutmacher, D. Cochrane and N. Bottani (eds) *In Pursuit of Equity in Education*. Dordrecht: Kluwer.

Berliner, D. (2001) The John Dewey Lecture. Paper delivered at the American Educational Research Association, Seattle, April.

Berliner, D.C. and Biddle, B.J. (1995) *The Manufactured Crisis: Myths, Fraud and Attack on America's Public Schools*. Reading, MA: Perseus Books.

Black, P. and Wiliam, D. (1998) *Beyond the Black Box*. London: King's College.

Bracey, G. (2001) Test scores, creativity and global competitiveness, *New York Times*, 16 December.

Bramall, S. and White, J. (eds) (2000) *Why Learn Maths?* London: Institute of Education.

Castells, M. (1996) *The Network Society*. Oxford: Blackwell.

Castells, M. (1999) *End of Millennium*. Oxford: Blackwell.

Cheng, Y.E. (2001) Towards the third wave of education reforms in Hong Kong. Keynote speech at the International Forum on Education Reforms in the Asia-Pacific Region, 14–16 February.

Coleman, J.S., Campbell, E.Q., Hobson, C.J., McPartland, J., Mood, A.M., Wienfeld, F.D. and York, R.L. (1966) *Equality of Educational Opportunity*. Washington, DC: Office of Education.

Creemers, B. (2001) Educational effectiveness research – some issues related to the discussion. Paper delivered at the International Conference on Knowledge Economy and Educational Development, Taipei, December.

Cuban, L. (2001) Improving urban schools in the 21st century: do's and don'ts or advice to true believers and skeptics of whole school reform. Paper presented at the OERI Summer Institute, CSR Grantees Conference, July.

Demeuse, M., Crahay, M. and Monseur, C. (2001) Efficiency and equity, in W. Hutmacher, D. Cochrane and N. Bottani (eds) *In Pursuit of Equity in Education*. Dordrecht: Kluwer.

Elliott, J. (1996) School effectiveness research and its critics: alternative visions of schooling, *Cambridge Journal of Education*, 26(2): 199–224.

Elmore, R.F. (2000) *Building a New Structure for School Leadership*. Washington, DC: The Albert Shanker Institute.

European Commission (2000) *European Report on Quality of School Education: Sixteen Quality Indicators*. (Report based on the work of the Working Committee on Quality Indicators). Brussels: European Commission.

Fielding, M. (1997) Beyond school effectiveness and school improvement: lighting the slow fuse of possibility, in J. White and M. Barber (eds) *Perspectives on School Effectiveness and School Improvement*. London: Institute of Education.

Fielding, M. and Bragg, S. (2003) *Students as Researchers: Making a Difference*. Cambridge: Pearson.

Frost, D., Durrant, J. and Head, M. (2000) *Teacher-led School Improvement*. London: Routledge.

Fullan, M. *et al.* (2001) Watching and Learning 2: OISE/UT evaluation of the implementation of the national literacy and numeracy strategies. Second annual report. London: DfES for Ontario Institute for Studies in Education, University of Toronto.

Goodman, P. (1971) *Compulsory Miseducation*. Harmondsworth, UK: Penguin Books.

Gray, J., Hopkins, D., Reynolds, D., Wilcox, B., Farrell, S. and Jesson, D. (1999) *Improving Schools: Performance and Potential*. Buckingham, UK: Open University Press.

Grisay, A. (1999) Comment mesurer l'efficacité du système scolaire sur les inégalités entre élèves? (How to measure school systems in terms of pupil inequalities) in D. Meuret (ed.) *La Justice du Système Éducatif.* Louvain: De Boeck Université.

Groundwater-Smith, S. (1999) Students as researchers: two Australian case studies. Paper presented at the British Education Research Association, University of Sussex, September.

Harris, J.R. (1998) *The Nurture Assumption.* London: Bloomsbury.

Hentig, H.v. (2001) *Warum Muss Ich in der Schule Gehen?* Munich: Care Hanser Verlag.

Hofstede, G. (1980) *Culture's Consequences: International Differences in Work-related Values.* Beverly Hills, CA: Sage.

Holt, J. (1976) *The Underachieving School.* Harmondsworth, UK: Pelican.

Illich, I. (1971) *Deschooling Society.* New York: Harper & Row.

Jencks, C.S., Smith, M., Ackland, H., Bane, M.J., Cohen, D., Gintis, H., Heyns, B. and Micholson, S. (1972) *Inequality: A Reassessment of the Effect of Family and Schooling in America.* New York: Basic Books.

Kerr, D., Lines A., Blenkinsop, S. and Schagen, I. (2001) quoted in A. Kirton and H. Brighouse, *Compulsory Citizenship Education In England.* London: Institute of Education.

Kozol, J. (1968) *Death at an Early Age.* Harmondsworth, UK: Penguin Books.

Labaree, D.F. (1997) *How to Succeed in School Without Really Learning: The Credentials Race in American Education.* New Haven, CT: Yale University Press.

Levin, B. (1998) The educational requirement for democracy, *Curriculum Inquiry*, 28(1): 57–79.

Levin, B. (1999) Putting students at the centre of educational reform, *Journal of Educational Change* (paper submitted).

Levine, D.U. and Lezotte, L.W. (1990) *Unusually Effective Schools: A Review and Analysis of Research and Practice.* Madison, WI: National Centre for Effective Schools Research and Development.

Lo, L.N.K. (1999) Knowledge, education and development in Hong Kong and Shanghai, *Education Journal*, 27(1): 55–91.

MacBeath, J. (1999) *Schools Must Speak for Themselves: The Case for School Evaluation.* London: Routledge.

MacBeath, J. and Mortimore, P. (eds) (2001) *Improving School Effectiveness.* Buckingham, UK: Open University Press.

MacBeath, J. and Stoll, L. (2001) The change equation: capacity for improvement, in J. MacBeath and P. Mortimore (eds) *Improving School Effectiveness.* Buckingham, UK: Open University Press.

MacBeath, J., Myers, K. and Demetriou, H. (2001) The need to transform teachers' perceptions of pupils' capabilities to discuss and make decisions about teaching and learning. Paper delivered at the British Educational Research Association conference, Leeds, 15 September.

MacBeath, J., Demetriou, H., Rudduck, J. and Myers, K. (2003) *Consulting Pupils: A Toolkit for Teachers.* Cambridge: Pearson.

Martin, P. (1997) *The Sickening Mind*. London: Flamingo.

Meuret, D. (2001) A system of equity indicators for educational systems, in W. Hutmacher, D. Cochrane and N. Bottani (eds) *In Pursuit of Equity in Education*. Dordrecht: Kluwer.

Ministry of Education and Science (2002) *A School for All*. Stockholm: Ministry of Education and Science.

Moos, L. and MacBeath, J. (2001) *Skolen Kan Svaren vor sig Selv*. Copenhagen: Dafolo.

National Commission on Excellence (1983) *Nation at Risk?* Washington, DC: Department of Education.

Orfield, G. and Eaton, S.E. (1996) *Dismantling Desegregation*. New York: New Press.

Otero, G., Chambers-Otero, S. and Sparks, R. (2000) *Relational Learning*. Melbourne: Hawker Brownlow.

Pearson, A. (1992) Teacher education in a democracy, *Educational Philosophy and Theory*, 24: 83–92.

Pharr, S.J. and Putnam, D. (eds) (2000) *Disaffected Democracies: What's Troubling the Trilateral Countries?* Princeton, NJ: Princeton University Press.

Postman, N. and Weingartner, C. (1970) *Teaching as a Subversive Activity*. Harmondsworth, UK: Penguin.

Putnam, R. (1999) *Bowling Alone: The Collapse and Revival of American Community*. New York: Touchstone.

Reichert, M.C. (2000) Disturbances of difference, in L. Weis and M. Fine (eds) *Construction Sites: Excavating Race, Class and Gender among Urban Youth*. New York, Teachers College Press.

Reimer, E. (1971) *School is Dead*. Harmondsworth, UK: Penguin Books.

Sammons, P. (1995) Gender, ethnic and socio-economic differences, attainment and progress: a longitudinal analysis of student achievement over 9 years, *British Educational Research Journal*, 21(4): 465–86.

Saunders, L. (2000) *Raising Attainment in Secondary Schools: A Handbook for Self-evaluation*. Slough, UK: National Foundation for Educational Research.

Schratz, M. (1997) *Using Photographs in School Self-evaluation*. Dundee, UK: CIDREE.

Silberman, C. (1973) *Crisis in the Classroom*. New York: Vintage Books.

Slee, R., Weiner, G. and Tomlinson, S. (eds) (1998) *School Effectiveness for Whom? Challenges to the School Effectiveness and School Improvement Movement*. London: Falmer Press.

Smith, D. and Tomlinson, S. (1989) *The School Effect: A Study of Multiracial Comprehensives*. London: Policy Studies Institute.

Stoll, L. and Fink, D. (1996) *Changing Our Schools: Linking School Effectiveness and School Improvement*. Buckingham, UK: Open University Press.

Stoll, L., Earle, L. and Fink, D. (forthcoming) *It's About Learning: What's in it for Schools?* London: Routledge.

Sung-Sik Kim (2002) The influence of private education on schooling in Korea: high academic achievement and 'school collapse'. Paper presented at the ICSEI 2002 conference, Copenhagen, 3–7 January.

Swaffield, S. (2002) Contextualising the work of the critical friend. Paper presented at the 15th International Congress on School Effectiveness and Improvement, Copenhagen, January.

Szreter, S. (2001) *Social Capital*. Glasgow: Roundtable.

Tang, C. (1996) Collaborative learning: the latent dimension in Chinese students' learning, in D.A. Watkins and J. Biggs (eds) *The Chinese Learner: Cultural, Psychological and Contextual Influences*, pp. 183–204. Hong Kong: Comparative Education Research Centre, University of Hong Kong.

Teddlie, C., Reynolds, D. and Pol, S. (2000) Current Topics and approaches in school effectiveness research, in C. Teddlie and D. Reynolds (eds) *The International Handbook of School Effectiveness Research*. London: Falmer.

Thomas, S., Smees, R., Sammons, P. and Roberston, P. (2001) Attainment, progress and value-added, in J. MacBeath, and P. Mortimore (eds) *Improving School Effectiveness*. Buckingham, UK: Open University Press.

Tooley, J. (2000) *Reclaiming Education*. London: Cassell.

Townsend, T. (1996) The self-managing school: miracle or myth? *Leading and Managing*, 2(3): 171–94.

Townsend, T. (2001) Improving school effectiveness for all students. Paper delivered at the International Conference on Knowledge Economy and Educational Development, Taipei, December.

Thrupp, M. (1999) *Schools Making a Difference: Let's Be Realistic*. Buckingham, UK: Open University Press.

Waiton, S. (2001) *Scared of the Kids?* Sheffield, UK: Sheffield Hallam University Press.

Ward, J.V. (2000) Raising resisters: the role of truth telling in the psychological development of Afro-American Girls, in L. Weis and M. Fine (eds) *Construction Sites: Excavating Race, Class and Gender among Urban Youth*. New York: Teachers College Press.

Watkins, C. (2001) Learning about learning improves performance, *NSIN Research Matters*, 13: 1–8.

Whitty, G. (1994) Subjects and themes in the secondary school curriculum, *Research Papers in Education*, 9(2): 159–81.

Willms, J.D. (1985) The balance thesis: contextual effects of ability on pupils' 'O' grade examination results, *Oxford Review of Education*, 11(1): 33–41.

Willms, J.D. (1997) *Parental Choice and Education Policy*, CES Briefing, No. 12, August.

Zeldin, T. (1996) *An Intimate History of Humanity*. New York: Torch Books.

2 Reforming for democratic schooling
Learning for the future not yearning for the past

Kathryn Riley

Introduction

Over a century ago, John Dewey railed against 'the ordinary school room with its rows of ugly desks placed in geometrical order'. In his view, this typical classroom organisation was made for listening and marked 'the dependency of one mind upon another' (Dewey 1900: 173). If Dewey were to visit many of our classrooms today, he would be disappointed at how little has changed – and yet education reform is high on the political agenda of many countries.

There is a range of social, economic and political explanations for the growing interest of governments across the globe in education reform. Equally too, as I shall suggest in this chapter, there are many pressing reasons why citizens – as well as their governments – should be engaged in the debate about the nature of those reforms.[1]

The basis of the argument put forward here is twofold. First, if we are to meet the challenges of the twenty-first century, we will need to confront some of the assumptions which govern how we think about effectiveness, how we attempt to 'measure' what goes on in classrooms and schools, and also reconsider the ways in which education reforms are developed and implemented. Second, we will need to shift the focus of the debate from schools to *schooling*: a term which reflects the broader environment for 'learning', recognising that learning takes place beyond the school gate and that teaching can exceed the confines of the classroom. If this shift is to take place, we will need to re-evaluate key values and goals and develop frameworks which are more inclusive of the needs of the disengaged and marginalised.

In order to explore these issues, and reappraise some of the cherished assumptions about how schools and classrooms function, I have drawn on the experience of a number of disaffected students, as well as changes in education policy and practice across a number of countries and contexts. My exploration is organised around five basic questions about reform:

- Reforming – why?
- Reforming – how?
- Reforming – what?
- Reforming – for whom?
- Reforming – for what?

Reforming – why?

Governments: controlling the agenda or paving the way?

Schools reflect the aspirations of communities, both for individuals within that community, as well as for the community as a whole. Thus questions about 'who' should control education and determine 'what' is to be taught, 'how' and 'by whom' are the source of ongoing debate and dispute, as well as periodic bouts of compromise between governments/states and various stakeholder groups, be they parents, religious communities, teachers or trade unions. Some years ago, I posed the question 'Whose school is it anyway?' in a book which explored the options available to an incoming UK Labour government after many years of Conservative control (Riley 1998). The challenge, as I saw it, was whether the new government could resist further expansion of state control of education – it could not.

There are many pressing reasons today why governments – not just in the UK but elsewhere – need to reflect on the balance to be struck between state responsibility for education and state control. In an increasingly complex global climate, the temptation for governments to exert control appears irresistible. However, there are a number of reasons why they should resist: some to do with 11 September 2001, and some to do with the nature of democracy. The events of 11 September, coupled with the speed and complexity of globalisation and the impact of new technologies, give a new urgency to the resolution of the question 'Whose school is it anyway?'

Global alliances and global uncertainties

Much has been written about the global, technological and societal contexts in which teaching and learning in the twenty-first century will take place. Globalisation and global capitalism have combined in ways that have enabled transnational companies to override the power and authority of states. There are also many networks and alliances that transcend borders, creating new cross-national alliances and providing a complex web of opportunities, not only for global activists (anti-global, environmental, anti-Third World debt, trade union), but also for global terrorists.

While globalisation and global capitalism are strongly connected, John Gray (2002: 25) reminds us that we need to distinguish between globalisation and the spread of free markets. The latter, he argues, is a political project less than a decade old, while the former began in the late nineteenth century, with the introduction of transatlantic cables: 'Properly understood, globalisation means nothing more than the increasing interconnections of world events, created by technologies which abolish or curtail time and distance' (p. 27). In the context of 11 September, however, he suggests that the USA is losing its interest in pursuing the free-market ideology, concentrating instead on the threats to US security, as unchecked globalisation creates a 'semi-anarchic environment' which threatens 'even the strongest of states' (p. 27).

Thus there are many other uncertainties about the global context for education which are magnified not only by 11 September but also by the IT revolution. Globalisation feeds, and is fed by, the demand for knowledge and information. The free accessibility of information on the scale offered by the internet and interactive technology promotes the flow of both information and disinformation: knowledge that is anti-educational, as well as knowledge that is educational, information that is anti-social, as well as information that is beneficial to society (MacBeath *et al.* 1996, 1998; Riley 2000). Globalisation may create a universal dress code for young people, but it also erodes previous cultural or linguistic distinctions between countries (Albrow 1994). Access to knowledge and information may widen young people's horizons, but it also puts them into contact with ideas and attitudes which may be at variance with those of their family or local community.

Globalisation and technology go hand in hand, as the events of 11 September demonstrated. Mobile phones came into their own for many caught up in the tragedy. Media accounts of the events entered people's homes across the globe within minutes of the first attack on New York. However, despite the global media context, the messages were not universal, forcing us to recognise that in a global context, populations are exposed to competing accounts of reality in relation to the same events. How people interpret those events is shaped by prior beliefs, experiences and expectations. Globalisation may offer opportunities to accelerate learning and speed the pace of change, but it also generates new tensions and dilemmas. Technology itself is both a unifier and a divider: providing opportunities for some but creating a digital divide between those who have entrée and those who do not.[2]

The technological revolution

In this new uncertain, global and technological world many educators struggle not only with global tragedies (should schools be seen as havens from the global maelstrom, or as places for informed debate and discussion?) but also with technological challenges. Some educators are comfortable with interactive technology, others find it difficult to acknowledge the technological capacities and skills of their students, as well as the potential power of technology. Both challenge traditional notions of how teachers teach, and how pupils learn, and raise questions for policy makers and practitioners alike, about ways in which the technological revolution can be harnessed to support teaching and learning.

There are three questions to be answered about these technological challenges. The first is 'How can educators prepare the citizens of tomorrow for the new global and technological revolution?' The conventional response to this question is to focus on computer literacy – an obvious but limited response, as technology changes so fast. The second broader and more reflective question is to ask 'How can we focus on the young person as the "digital learner"?' This question recognises the connections between school- and non-school-based learning, particularly in relation to IT, as illustrated in Figure 2.1, taken from a recent publication (OECD 2001: 12).[3]

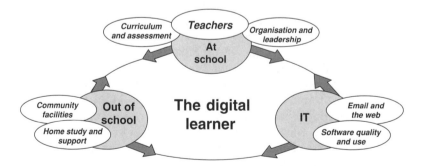

Figure 2.1 The digital learner
Source: OECD (2001)

However, the third and perhaps even more critical question is 'How can technology contribute to the creation of the kind of society we want to see?' The answer to this question raises many issues about education and democracy and takes us into the territory of value judgements. It also raises fundamental concerns about the nature and purpose of education, as well as who should determine its ends – teachers, government or other groups?

Reforming – how?

The participative approach

Karen Seashore Louis argues in the next chapter that the slogans which shape the education reforms of most countries are based on one of three competing theories of democracy: *liberal democracy* (democracy as individual opportunity); *social democracy* (democracy as social opportunities for groups); and *participatory democracy* (democracy as local voice and influence). She suggests that these three conceptualisations are embedded in national cultures and beliefs and contain very different answers to the question 'Whose school is it anyway?'

Underpinning liberal democracy, she argues, is the belief that schooling is largely the responsibility of the government, whose role it is to determine what the electorate will support. While social democracies also assume that the state should control education, the state's role is to redress imbalances and to ensure that vulnerable children are protected. The organisational premise underpinning participatory democracy is that participants are best able and positioned to determine goals.

The basis of the argument which I want to put forward here is that the contextual challenges outlined in the previous section create a new urgency for education reform, as well as a pressing need to incorporate broader democratic concepts into the reform process. Democracy as local voice and influence comes into its own, aligned to approaches to reform which encourage ownership and involvement in ways that will enable people to make sense of the uncertain world they inhabit, by contributing more extensively and intensively to the communities in which they live. This is not to reject out of hand social democratic notions of redressing inequality but to suggest that: the state is limited in what it can do; and the notion of the state as the sole arbiter of truth and justice can disempower communities which are already facing major upheavals.

In the context of educational reform, the notion of democracy as participation raises issues about the practice of democracy. If we are to develop democratic competencies, how can we model democratic participation through all the different levels and layers of an education system? If we are to prepare young people for an increasingly uncertain and hazardous world in which they will need to be able to discriminate between competing truths and realities, how do we involve them as students in the myriad of decisions which influence their learning environment? If we are to equip teachers to meet both the known and unknown challenges of the future, how do we engage them in the process and dialogue of education reform and change? If we are to enable communities to shape their local environments, how do we engage them in redefining what *is*, as well as what *might be*?

Democratic participation is part of the answer to these questions and needs to be considered not just as an outcome from an education system but as a process goal. By this I mean that the extent and nature of democratic participation may be viewed as an intermediate indicator which gives some signal of the needs and aspirations of communities. If we accept this premise, then we need to think about how education change is conceived and implemented, as well as the ways in which the processes of teaching and learning take place on a daily basis.

The inclusive approach

Much has been written about the nature of educational reform, but it is worth emphasising that successful reforms depend on three inter-connected elements (Riley 2000):

- the skills, capacity and commitment of educators within school, and at the local system level;
- the enthusiasm and commitment of parents, pupils and teachers;
- the ability of politicians to create the right legislative framework.

All too often, the emphasis is on the last of these three elements, although getting the policy right is only part of the jigsaw. Reforms tend to fail for a number of reasons. One is the tendency, as Sarason has described it, to focus on the supposed villains of the piece, 'inadequate teachers, irresponsible parents, irrelevant or inadequate curricula, unmotivated students . . . and an improvement-defeating bureaucracy' (1990: 13). Education reforms are more likely to work when teachers, parents, pupils and administrators are seen as part of the solution, not part of the problem. If countries are to implement the kinds of changes that they envisage, they will need the active cooperation of all these groups.

As governments around the world become even more engaged in the education reform business, teachers find themselves in the firing line, caught between the often competing demands of different stakeholders. On one side are pupils and parents who are more questioning of the role and authority of teachers than in the past, and on the other side are governments who demand higher standards and greater accountability. The student population is changing and becoming more diverse culturally and linguistically, with greater numbers of pupils with special educational needs. Sorting through these various challenges requires high levels of cooperation among teachers, pupils and policy makers; ongoing professional pathways and opportunities for teachers and other paraprofessionals; and an approach to educational reform which embraces new ways of bringing teachers, families, pupils and communities into the reform process.

A second reason for the failure of education reforms is the tendency to divide reforms into two mental 'black boxes', one called 'structural reform' and the other called 'cognition' or 'learning' (Riley 2000). The policies in the structural reform box focus on major organisational arrangements (how to build more schools, expand teacher supply, restructure pre-service training etc.). Most of the time and energy tends to go into the structural reform box, as the political stakes are so high. Yet in the last analysis, reforms will be judged by the effectiveness of their impact on the cognition or learning box – that is, the extent to which *real* changes in teaching and learning take place.

Substantive change in what teachers actually do in their classrooms has been the most elusive goal of school improvement efforts (Elmore 1995; Tyack and Cuban 1995; Louis *et al.* 1999).[4] If reforms are to succeed, teachers are required not only to change *what* they teach, but also the assumptions and beliefs that guide *how* they teach – what Toole (2000) has called the teachers' 'grammar of learning'. This again forces us to reflect on how teachers can become part of the reform process, and the prominence and starting points of reform.

A bottom-up approach

Evidence across many countries and contexts suggests that bottom-up reforms are likely to have a greater impact and to be sustained over time than top-down ones. A cross-national study of change and improvement in England and Singapore, for example, found that successful efforts to achieve school-based improvement in very different contexts had a number of common elements: motivating staff; focusing improvements on teaching and learning; enhancing the physical environment; and changing the culture of the school. The researchers involved in the study offered three key messages for policy makers (Mortimore *et al.* 2000: 143).

- improvement techniques must fit with the grain of the society, rather than go against it – indiscriminate borrowing from other cultures may not achieve the desired results;
- in themselves, resources do not guarantee improvement but they help convince staff, parents and students that their society believes in the school and is prepared to invest in it;
- change has to be carried out by the school itself.

Examples of bottom-up approaches to reform can be found in a variety of contexts. Guinea, for example, has developed a range of strategies designed to bring teachers and communities into the reform process. As part of this approach, it has embarked on a project designed to improve student learning by supporting teacher development: the Small Grants, Staff Development and School Improvement (PPSE) project. PPSE starts from the local school community. Teachers and school directors are encouraged to form teams and adopt a problem-solving approach aimed at identifying the barriers to learning, sharing these perceptions with the local community and agreeing local priorities about what needs to be done and how. The PPSE framework has created a common language for teachers and other educators to address diverse educational challenges, and has generated considerable enthusiasm (Riley *et al.* 2000; Schwille *et al.* 2000).

The process of debate and discussion with teachers, parents and communities in Guinea has been used to develop criteria about minimum standards for quality around the core elements of what constitutes an *École de Qualité Fondamentale*. The criteria summarise expectations about the appropriate levels of provision which should be available to children in primary schools across the whole country. These criteria have been expressed as a number of indicators which attempt to define a set of values at two different levels:

- *Le Niveau Acceptable*: what constitutes acceptable practice and performance. Anything below or beyond these norms must be considered unacceptable and in urgent need of improvement.
- *Le Niveau Visé*: future targets to ensure quality improvement.[5]

It is this type of local engagement in the goals and outcomes of reform which will help to generate not just change but improvement, and in ways that reflect shared societal goals and aspirations.

The Guinea experience has much to teach us. It shows the strengths of an approach which is bottom-up, designed to enable teachers to reflect on their thinking and practice and linked to a broader-based view of what quality currently looks like, as well as what it might be. However, the process of engagement is not necessarily an easy one. Different groups have their own views and perceptions and the notion of what makes a 'good' school is a social construct. Thus a reform process which is based on democratic participation would need to question national and local constructions and beliefs about:

- what makes a good teacher/good teaching/a good education experience/a good school;
- what count as good learning outcomes;
- what are the views of different stakeholder groups (politicians, administrators, teachers, parents, pupils).

It would also need to explore any discrepancies in views between different regions, or religious or ethnic groups.[6] Such an approach generates debate about current and future aspirations and becomes, in itself, part of the reform and change process by helping to define the future goals of schooling, what quality looks like in a particular context and the pathways to quality improvement.

Reforming – what?

Governments not only have choices about *how* they go about reform, but also about *what* they chose to focus on. Approaches to reform differ between countries and also change within countries over time:

- some approaches are *systemic* (focusing on the problems of fragmentation and lack of coordination between policies);
- others focus on *restructuring* (addressing the problems of out-moded school organisation);
- still others, particularly in developing contexts, focus on *expansion* (increased enrolment, wider access etc.).

Approaches to reform are also culturally specific, shaped by ideology and history, as well as by social and economic imperatives. Most reform initiatives contain many of the same ingredients, such as curriculum or teacher education reform. Most acknowledge, to a greater or lesser degree, the global and technological imperatives of the twenty-first century. However, governments or states differ in the *levers* which they select to kick-start or steer the reform process, as well as in the *drivers* – the reform imperatives.

Looking across developed and developing country contexts, governments have used a range of levers. These include the introduction of *standardised testing* (e.g. in the USA); the development of *external audit* and *inspection procedures* and the introduction of *accountability mechanisms* (in the UK); the expansion of *large-scale teacher development programmes* (in Uganda); the involvement of *parents and communities* (in Columbia and Escuela Nueva); and the creation of *school-based school improvement projects* (in Guinea). These approaches are not mutually exclusive, and mature education systems are likely to include all or most of these elements. However, there are likely to be distinctive differences in emphasis, in starting points and in expectations about outcomes.

In Figure 2.2 I have summarised the core components of an education reform process under five core headings: the system drivers, the levers

---

1 **System drivers:** the major pressures for change within the system, the social, ideological and political forces which create the climate and imperatives for reform of the system and its overall direction

2 **Levers for change:** the specific mechanisms chosen to implement the changes, which tend to include the following:

- capacity building
- curriculum
- assessment
- evaluation (external and self-evaluation)
- accountability and standards agenda
- funding mechanisms
- innovations in teaching and learning and in raising achievement

3 **Partnerships for change:** identification of the stakeholders and the extent to which they have been brought into the change process

4 **The achievements:** assessment of what has been achieved so far during the current cycle of reform, along with any supporting evidence

5 **The challenges:** those which have still to be met, the further reforms yet to be realised, as well as the additional reforms required as a consequence of changes which have already been made

---

Figure 2.2 Five core components of education reform

for change, the partnerships for change, the achievements and the challenges (Riley 2001a, 2001b). These five aspects are not intended to be all-embracing of a country's programme of educational reform, nor are there always clear demarcations between categories. However, they form a broad framework which offers a useful perspective at one point in time. The drivers – the reform imperatives – may alter because of political, economic or social factors. Other partners may come on board at different stages in the reform process. The achievements and challenges may also change as new accomplishments and problems emerge.

This framework is useful in highlighting some important differences between the ways in which education reforms are conceived and put in place and the options which governments have available to them, not only in *what* they chose to reform but in *how* they go about it. The following two examples are from Uruguay and the State of Parana (in Brazil).

Uruguay's system drivers are based on clearly articulated and long-standing policy goals about social equity. As in many other countries, Uruguay has used assessment as a lever for change, developing a national census-based student assessment system as a tool for *social accountability*, rather than as a mechanism for *consumer accountability* (as has been the case in the UK). Data from the national assessment programme is used to guide improvements in teaching practice and to reveal the impact of sociocultural factors (i.e. levels of poverty, mothers' level of education) on education outcomes. By adopting such an approach, the government acknowledged its own responsibility for the conditions of education.

The drivers for reform in Parana are shaped by national Brazilian goals, as well as local imperatives. The chief secretary of state described the main state driver in the following terms: 'All children in school, learning and completing 11 years of school in 11 years'.[7] Parana has utilised a capacity building approach as its main lever for change, investing heavily in a programme which aims to reach *all* educators, not just teachers, and to encourage the development of leadership skills throughout the education system. Teachers are entitled to a minimum of 40 hours per year of training and directors (headteachers), 80 hours. Staff are released from their day-to-day responsibilities and all costs are covered by the state. The Capacity Building Programme is brought together under the 'Universidade do Professor' – a virtual university, with an administrative and strategic base in the Education Secretariate of the government of Parana. The heart of the Universidade do Professor is Faxinal do Céu, a village in central Parana with a rich and creative learning environment and the 'brain child' of the current state governor (Riley 2001a; Riley *et al.* 2001).

The capacity building lever in Parana (designed to show that teachers can make a difference) has succeeded in offering them a range of professionally rewarding experiences. It demonstrated that teachers' professional judgements are valued and helped create a common language to talk about educational issues. Uruguay's approach to assessment has enabled a focus on examination performance which is not in the teacher 'blame' mode. In both cases (Uruguay and Parana) the objective has been to develop a social partnership which involves teachers.

Reforming – for whom?

Nobel prize winner Amartya Sen reminds us that in our world of overall opulence, millions of people remain 'unfree', not technically slaves (although some still are), but denied basic freedoms because of their poverty and their lack of access to civil liberties, health or education (Sen 1999). While the right to good quality education is one that many people take for granted today, along with the right to good health and a reasonable living standard, the reality is that many children and young people are denied that right. The notion of the right to learn is a powerful one in the context of education for all but also in national contexts in which all children have the right to attend school, without cost, throughout their statutory years of schooling. In a range of industrialised contexts, children and young people have become disadvantaged by the *process* of schooling: as a result of the cumulative impact of the demands on teachers, the competitive pressures generated by national demands as well as the varying needs of students themselves.

In a collaborative two-year project on disenfranchised young people in Lancashire in the North of England, we listened to many voices, including local policy makers and professionals involved in running projects with disaffected young people, as well as teachers, headteachers, parents and pupils (Riley *et al.* 2002). Through listening to the voices of the young people themselves – experts in their own schooling experience – we can learn much about how to reshape schooling.

Fragmented, inconsistent and interrupted learning

Schools operate on the basis of a number of assumptions. One is that young people come to school on time, daily and with no interruptions to their learning. The reality, of course, is far removed from this. For many pupils, learning is a fragmented, inconsistent and interrupted experience. There are a number of reasons for this, some to do with the absences and attitudes of students themselves, others to do with teachers' absences. Numerous pupils in our study experienced high teacher turnover and repetition, and gaps in their learning experience because of this. Many interpreted the failure of the school to find a suitable replacement teacher as a personal rejection.

Students also missed out on learning opportunities because of school discipline policies. Some were put 'on ice' – in 'isolation', a room to which pupils were sent following a number of warnings about their behaviour. Children on ice were separated from their peers, and in their view became outcasts from the daily life of the school, unable to move forward.

Fragmentation in the learning process also occurred because of pupils' own absence from school. Many of our interviewees were 'in and out' of school for a variety of reasons – and re-entry was a major stumbling block. Erratic attendance led to sarcastic comments from teachers such as, 'Oh you have finally decided to join us today then, have you?' One boy, returning after a long absence was told that he 'should just go back home', which he did. Pupils described re-entry as a lonely and isolated business, and reintegration as difficult. One form teacher 'welcomed' back a student, a long-term truant, by encouraging the class to clap – slowly. The extent to which pupils were able to keep up with the flow of work depended, to a large degree, on the goodwill of their friends, from whom they copied notes.

Relationships matter

We found that pupils' views about school were shaped by a number of key people and events. Relationships with teachers were key (see Figure 2.3).

Many of the pupils we met were vulnerable for a number of reasons – including major pressures at home, as well as experiencing acute learning difficulties – and were susceptible to the highs and lows of school life. Encounters with one or two hectoring teachers could tip the balance in their behaviour and send them spiralling down the path of exclusion, or truanting from school. Equally, the support and endorsement of key teachers who understood their needs could keep them on track. Pupils were particularly critical of teachers who were rigid, lacked understanding and were unfair, or were determined that 'everything must be right'. But they also recognised the tremendous demands on teachers, and the ways in which their behaviour, and that

'Good' teachers were:	'Bad' teachers were:
• helpful and supportive	• mean and unfair
• willing to take the time to explain material in depth	• unwilling to help or explain material and ideas beyond instruction
• friendly and personable	• judgemental of pupils' parents and siblings
• understanding of pupils and knew their subject well	• routine and unchanging in their teaching styles and methods
• able to use a variety of teaching styles and innovative approaches	• inflexible and disrespectful of pupils
• fair, and had equal standards and expectations for pupils, regardless of their test scores	• unaware of, and unsympathetic to, pupils' personal problems
• willing to reward pupils for progress	• physically intimidating and verbally abusive

Figure 2.3 'Good' and 'bad' teachers

of other pupils, contributed to the build up of tensions in the classroom. Many pupils described teachers as 'stressed out by teaching', observing that teachers' jobs were 'not easy these days'.

The 'failure' label

Many students expressed the view that once they, and other students, had got into a downward spiral of bad behaviour, exclusion and non-attendance, the chances of improving their prospects in the school were almost nil. Some claimed that they had been labelled as potential troublemakers on the basis of the track record of brothers and sisters, or in several cases because of the behaviour of their own parents as past pupils in the school.

The children typically saw themselves as being at the bottom of the heap, labelled by teachers as 'thick', 'stupid' and not wanted in the school. For many of the young people we interviewed, school was a profoundly sad and depressing experience. The images and depictions were powerful, suggesting 'I am very sad', 'stressed out', 'lonely', 'depressed', 'on my own'. Many of the images are bleak, picturing isolated children and shouting teachers. A reoccurring image is of school as a prison from which children continually try to escape.

The authority figures (the teachers) loomed large and seemed to have few connections with the young people on a personal level or through classroom interactions. The children themselves often appeared as lost, small voices crying for help, caught in a cycle of events and circumstances which they felt unable to influence. Once they had been labelled as difficult, once they were on the downward spiral of bad behaviour (conflict with teachers or truancy) it was difficult to escape. Their alienation was increased by a feeling that teachers and head-teachers wanted to 'get them out' of school.

Many pupils were deeply offended by the day-to-day physical environment which they encountered: 'the toilets are disgusting, they stink', 'there's no paper', 'it's horrible and unhygienic', were typical comments and occurred as images in their depictions of school life. Many described the dining area as being uncongenial and unwelcoming: 'it's really scruffy; the food is slopped onto a plate'. The poor physical school environment was interpreted as the school's lack of respect for pupils.

What's school got to do with learning?

Few pupils regarded school as a place for growing, learning new information or expanding their future options. Schooling was described as a grim and painstaking experience which had to be got through. 'Hanging out with your mates' was one of the few saving graces. School was also a place where pupils (particularly if they were 'different' or gay) could be bullied or ridiculed by their peers and generally ostracised – a process which could be deeply painful.

We asked our colleagues from Lancashire who worked with us to write their perceptions of the three main issues which had emerged from the student panels. One female education welfare officer described her experience in the following terms:

> The main point that will stay with me is the fact that many of the young people recognise that their behaviour needs to change but cannot envisage the process of being able to change. Their behaviour (and goals) are based on how staff expect them to behave. There is a major problem of communication between families and schools, but no one appears to recognise the problems, or be able to assist. The whole group had major communications problems with the teaching staff. They felt that teachers gave orders, did not treat them as individuals, and did not give them any space to be able to discuss their problems.

For many children on the margins, schooling is a deeply boring experience which can also be hazardous and demeaning. By and large, this is not because teachers are uncommitted to the needs of disaffected children, but because both teachers and pupils are locked into an education system which gives them little room for manoeuvre. The over-busy national policy agenda, characterised by repeated policy waves, appears slow to learn the lessons from previous reforms and has a tendency to mistake change for progress. Our current structures seem to be designed to create a blame culture which leaves troublesome children sad and alienated.

What do disaffected young people have to teach us?

We learned many lessons from working with disaffected young people, all of which are critical to our thinking about the nature of schooling in the future. Much of what they have to say is about the school climate and the nature of the relationships they have there. There is a demand for schools to be more open and more democratic. Disaffected young people, in particular, feel that they are not partners in their education experience. Their specific requests for the future include:

- smaller classes;
- more say for students in how schools are run;
- teachers who listen *to* pupils rather than talk *at* them;
- teachers who are more aware of the problems students face outside school;
- encouragement for teachers and pupils to respect each other;
- help with schoolwork provided to pupils who have missed school;
- more informal ways of learning offered both inside and outside school;
- more challenging lessons;
- improved physical conditions.

What is clear is that *relationships matter*. Mutual respect is key: pupil for teacher and teacher for pupil.[8] We concluded that the key to change lies in rethinking the nature of teaching and learning and recognising the fragmented nature of schooling, rather than focusing too narrowly on policies which aim to deal with poor student behaviour. We also observed that for many pupils school was a joyless experience.

For many children and young people, schooling is also a fragmented process. The evidence from our study is that practitioners need to be given the opportunity to experiment with new and radical ways of organising teaching and learning. Some of these may test the boundaries of the school day, or week, or even our concept of what a school looks like. There also needs to be an attitudinal shift on the part of governments and a recognition of the ways in which teachers can help shape policy, rather than always being shaped *by* it. Trust is needed to help bring about a shift in power relations between government and schools, and between teachers, pupils and parents.

Reforming – for what?[9]

I began this chapter by referring to the works of John Dewey and his concerns of over a century ago about the restrictive ways in which classrooms were structured. Dewey focused on the notion of children's learning as a process of problem solving and proposed a democratic pedagogy in which the child was viewed as an active agent in their own learning. In *Democracy and Education* (1912) he challenged what Robin Alexander has described as 'the prevailing pedagogy of fast cramming' and argued instead for an education which fostered 'reflection and scientific enquiry'. Dewey saw this as being 'congruent with the way a democracy should develop' (Alexander 2000: 112).

In the closing days of the Second World War, Arnold McNair was given the task by the British government, then led by Winston Churchill, of looking at the supply, recruitment and training of teachers. The McNair Report argued that if the country was to create a 'wise democracy' in the post-Hitler world, then it would need to recruit people of the highest calibre into teaching. Teaching required more than knowledge of subject matter. Teachers needed to be able to interpret the meaning of complex changes and enable young people to be able to discriminate and not be 'an easy prey to sensations and cheap appeals'. The Report concluded that the teaching profession had a strong social purpose and should be placed at the heart of the post-war reconstruction of society (Riley 1998). How do these issues of values and vision play out in our contemporary context (White 2000)? How do we strengthen democratic competencies through education and through the process of education reform? How do we develop forms of leadership that develop and support democracy (Riley and Louis 2000b)?

In the previous sections of this chapter I have described the range of factors which explain why education reforms need to continue apace, arguing that we need to embrace participative democracy, both in the ways that schooling is constructed on a daily basis and in how education is conceptualised and enacted as a process of reform. However, the key question is: 'reforming – for what?' The answer to that question has many component parts which probably include the following: reforming for democracy, reforming for learning, reforming for diversity, and reforming for complexity and uncertainty.

The extent to which the reforming zeal of governments will tackle these issues successfully depends on a range of factors: some to do with the policy options they chose to exercise; some to do with the extent to which parents, teachers and communities are engaged in the process of influencing future directions; and some to do with factors and circumstances that are as yet unknown. The range of possibilities (such as whether the digital divide will widen or narrow; the extent to which education will be driven by technology or will harness it to societal needs; the degree to which governments will create a climate of learning for all, or adopt policies which will increase fragmentation) will depend on a range of value choices, including whether education remains largely viewed as a public commodity, or becomes entirely seen as a private good (Caldwell 2000).

The focus on reforming for learning is critical. Although the current education discourse focuses on the need to move from teaching to learning, the gap between those discussions and the daily practices in many of our schools remains wide. We need to turn our attention, as Jerome Bruner and others have reminded us, to the interactive nature of learning and to teach, 'not to produce little libraries . . . but rather to get a student to think mathematically . . . to consider matters as an historian does, to take part in the process of knowledge getting' (Bruner 1968: 72). Creativity needs to be encouraged at every opportunity. Our aspiration needs to be for a rich and joyful learning environment which encourages 'mystery, chance and silence' (Pullman 2002).

The focus on learning is one of diversity, rather than uniformity, and is based on a recognition of the many and different ways in which learning takes place. Learning is a process, not a product, and is dependent on a range of factors, including what the individual brings to the learning experience, as well as societal values and aspirations. It is about culture and context, and cultural beliefs and aspirations combine to create different perceptions about the appropriateness of particular models of learning. A country's culture and history influence every aspect of public education, including the curriculum, school ethos, classroom relations and the very language used to describe teaching and learning (Alexander 2000).

My answer to the question 'reforming – for what?' is that we should be reforming to develop creative learning environments which

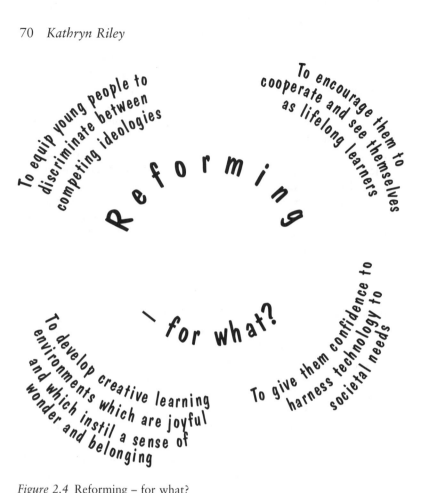

Figure 2.4 Reforming – for what?

are joyful and instil a sense of belonging; to equip young people to discriminate between competing ideologies; to encourage them to cooperate and see themselves as lifelong learners; to give them confidence to harness technology to societal needs (see Figure 2.4).

This is a notion of schooling as a tool for promoting global citizenship in a period of social, political and economic transformation, but it is also a recognition of the emancipatory nature of schooling – the ways in which it can spark a love of learning and a quest for knowledge which takes people through their lives. Reforming for the future is about developing an approach to reform which equips our children and young people to think, learn, reflect and work together. It is about resisting the temptation to hanker after a mythical golden age in which tractable children sat in uniform rows awaiting the next input of knowledge nuggets. Our yearning should not be for the past but for a future which, while full of uncertainty, is also filled with promise.

Notes

1 A parallel article to this one is to be published as 'Schooling the citizens of tomorrow', the title of a presentation at the ICSEI conference in Copenhagen, 6 January, 2002.

2 Internet access is dominated by the 19 per cent of the world's population who live in Organisation for Economic Cooperation and Development (OECD) countries, particularly the USA (UNICEF 1999).

3 With thanks to the author, Edwyn James (OECD) for this illustration (OECD 2001).

4 Both the school effectiveness and school improvement research fields have highlighted the centrality of teaching development in the pursuit of sustained school improvement (Harris 2001; Hopkins 2001), and the importance of teacher quality (Riley and Louis 2000b).

5 The published criteria covered a range of essentially practical elements related to educational provision including: the percentage of girl pupils attending primary school (40 per cent acceptable, 50 per cent targeted); class sizes (30–50 acceptable in rural areas, 40–60 in towns); minimum qualifications and initial training for teachers; a minimum number of textbooks per pupil according to their age range; a baseline number for student transfer into secondary schooling (60 per cent currently acceptable, 80 per cent envisaged); and the number of 'redoublements' to be kept below 10 per cent (Riley *et al.* 2000).

6 An understanding of these issues is critical to the reform process. Schools do not perceive reforms in a uniform way – much will depend on the local context, including the school's history or leadership (Riley 2000; Riley and Louis 2000a). A study of the impact of Nicaragua's decentralisation reforms, for example, indicated that parents, teachers and headteachers held divergent views about the goals and impact of the reforms. However, where these perceptions had been listened to and reconciled within the school community, the reform initiatives were much more likely to be successful (Fuller and Rivarola 1998).

7 This was during a discussion in Parana about the reform process (Riley *et al.* 2000).

8 This finding corresponds closely with a UK study on teacher effectiveness which suggests that 'respect for others underpins everything that effective teachers do' (Hay 2000: 1.3.7).

9 This final part of the chapter draws on the concluding section of 'Schooling the citizens of tomorrow' (see Note 1).

References

Albrow, M. (1994) Myths and realities. Professional Inaugural Lecture, Roehampton Institute, London, October.

Alexander, R. (2000) *Culture and Pedagogy: International Comparisons in Primary Education*. London: Blackwell.

Bruner, J.S. (1968) *Toward a Theory of Instruction*. New York: W.W. Norton.

Caldwell, B.J. (2000) A 'public good' test to guide the transformation of public education, *Journal of Educational Change*, 1(4): 307–29.

Dewey, J. (1900) *The School and Society*, Chicago: Chicago University Press.

Dewey, J. (1912) *Democracy and Education*. New York: MacMillan.

Elmore, R.F. (1995) Getting to scale with good educational practice, *Harvard Educational Review* 66(1): 1–26.

Fuller, B. and Rivarola, M. (1998) *Nicaragua's Experiment to Decentralise Schools: Views of Parents, Teachers and Directors*, working paper series on Impact Evaluation of Education Reforms, No. 5. Washington, DC: Development Economics Research Group, The World Bank.

Gray, J. (2002) The decay of the free market, *New Statesman*, 25 March: 25–7.

Harris, A. (2001) *School Improvement: What's in it for Schools?* London: Falmer Press.

Hay, McBer (2000) *Research into Teacher Effectiveness: A Model of Teacher Effectiveness*, report to the (UK) Department for Education and Employment (June). London: Department for Education and Employment.

Hopkins, D. (2001) *School Improvement for Real*. London: Falmer Press.

Louis, K.S., Toole, J. and Hargreaves, A. (1999) Rethinking school improvement, in J. Murphy and K.S. Louis (eds) *Handbook of Research on Educational Administration*, 2nd edn, pp. 251–75. San Francisco: Jossey Bass.

MacBeath, J. Moos, L. and Riley, K.A. (1996) Leadership in a changing world, in K. Leithwood, J. Chapman, D. Corson, P. Hallinger and A. Hart (eds) *International Handbook of Educational Leadership and Administration*. Dordrecht: Kluwer.

MacBeath, J., Moos, L. and Riley, K.A. (1998) Time for a change, in J. MacBeath (ed.) *Effective School Leadership Responding to Change*. London: Paul Chapman.

Mortimore, P., Gopinathan, S., Leo, S., Myers, K., Sharpe, L., Stoll, L. and Mortimore, J. (2000) *The Culture of Change: Case Studies of Improving Schools in Singapore and London*. London: Institute of Education, Bedford Papers.

OECD (2001) *Schooling for Tomorrow: Learning to Change ICT*. Paris: OECD.

Pullman, P. (2002) Give them a taste of honey, *Times Educational Supplement*, 8 February: 23.

Riley, K.A. (1998) *Whose School is it Anyway?* London: Falmer Press.

Riley, K.A. (2000) Leadership, learning and systemic reform, *Journal of Educational Change*, 1(1): 29–55.

Riley, K.A. (2001a) Re-ignite the flame, *Times Educational Supplement*, 17 August: 11.

Riley, K.A. (2001b) Levers for change and improvement: a framework for analysis. A contribution to the Marco de Aprendizagem Continua (MAC network).

Riley, K.A. and Louis, K.S. (2000a) What makes a good teacher? *New Statesman*, 2 October: xxxi.

Riley, K.A. and Louis, K.S. (2000b) *Leadership for Change and School Reform: International Perspectives*. London: Routledge/Falmer.

Riley, K.A., Rowles, D. and Edge, K. (2000) *Promoting Good Teaching and Learning: The Case of Guinea*, report to the Department for International Development. Washington, DC: World Bank, Effective Schools and Teachers Thematic Group.

Riley, K.A., Rose, J. and Watts, M. (2001) *Appraisal of Teacher Preparation and Development, Parana, Brazil*. Roehampton, UK: Centre for Educational Management, University of Surrey.

Riley, K.A. and Rustique Forrester, E., with Fuller, M., Rowles, D., Letch, R. and Docking, J. (2002) *Working with Disaffected Students: Why Students Lose Interest in School and What We Can Do About It*. London: Paul Chapman.

Sarason, S. (1990) *The Predictable Failure of Educational Reform*. San Francisco: Jossey Bass.

Schwille, J. and Dembélé, M. in collaboration with Adotevi, J. and Hamidou, T. *et al.* (2000) Teacher school improvement and professional development projects in Guinea: lessons learned from developing a nationwide program and issues in going to scale. Paper presented to the annual meetings of the Comparative and International Educational Society, San Antonio, Texas, March.

Sen, A. (1999) *Development as Freedom*. Oxford: Oxford University Press.

Toole, J.C. (2000) Implementing service-learning in K-8 schools: challenging the learning grammar and the organizational grammar of 'real school'. Paper presented at the AREA annual conference, New Orleans, 20 April.

Tyack, D. and Cuban, L. (1995) *Tinkering Toward Utopia: A Century of Public School Reform*. Cambridge, MA: Harvard University Press.

UNICEF (1999) Statistics, United Nations Children's Fund website. New York: UNICEF. www.unicef.org/magic/briefing/childmediaaccess.html, accessed 30 May, 2003.

White, R.C. (2000) *The School of Tomorrow*. Buckingham, UK: Open University Press.

3 Democratic values, democratic schools

Reflections in an international context[1]

Karen Seashore Louis

Setting the stage

Most nations are currently giving renewed attention to educational policy. Much of the discussion is strongly influenced by rhetoric about the 'real' goals of schooling, but all too often slogans, such as 'leave no child behind' and 'education for the global society' mask important underlying and conflicting questions of purpose. These slogans lack even the virtue of being code words for larger or more coherent conceptions of democratic education. The main purpose of this chapter is to render the concept of 'democratic schools' more problematic than resolved. The concept is subject to many meanings, even in countries that view themselves as 'modern democracies'. The multiple meanings of democracy become even more evident when we look at schools and schooling as an example. The implications for how we conceptualise effectiveness and approach improvement are far reaching.

I come to this topic reluctantly. However, democratic theories cast different shadows on contemporary educational issues that are at the heart of school effectiveness and improvement. Questions about how to organise schools so that they better serve the needs of teachers and students, or how to make education in disadvantaged settings more equitable, cannot be answered without reference to assumptions about democratic values. The educational slogans currently driving the debates over school reform tend to reflect back on one of three theories of democracy. Each slogan and theory seems attractive in isolation but is problematic when considered adjacent to competing models of democracy. In other words, political theories of democracy affect both a society's educational goals and the types of organisational structures that are best suited to achieving these goals.

Assumptions

Democracy has defeated various forms of totalitarianism, intellectually and practically, but we still live with largely implicit and poorly articulated assumptions about democratic schools and schooling. For example, an educator might articulate goals of choice and the ability of each student to rise to their level of attainment to murmuring approval from some audiences. These ideas would be received more cautiously, however, if we articulated the corresponding assumption that, although no student will be left behind, some will choose to stay behind while others will far exceed social expectations. Voices from research outlining fundamental dilemmas about the nature and purpose of schooling – and how these are reflected in debates about school organisation – are muddied because we are entangled in appealing, but competing, visions of democracy.

I begin with the premise that 'public schools . . . have functioned as ideological templates revealing and organizing national aspirations, myths, symbols, and standards' (Finkelstein 1984: 16). In taking democracy rather than governance or authority as my topic, I am taking a step outside of related reviews that have deeply influenced my thinking (White 1986; Murphy 2000). I enter this discussion humbly. I am a sociologist whose work has focused on the intersection of organisation theory and school reform, and not a political theorist or a philosopher. I do not pretend to have answers about democracy and *education*, having little to add to the contributions of Dewey and other curriculum theorists, but aim only to raise questions about what it means to talk about democratic *schools*.

Two additional concepts condition my remarks. First, culture is important as a partial determinant of the structure and outcomes of schooling. But culture has a meaning and use as messy as democracy (Firestone and Louis 2000). At its foundation it encompasses every aspect of our lives as social beings; its narrow use incorporates educational contexts in which it often represents specific value-laden goals. In between it presents an array of beliefs and motivations to be moulded, encouraged or suppressed. In education, culture conditions what teachers do in their classrooms, how individual schools play out the annual drama of creating learning environments and how the public assesses the successes and failures of its schools.

Second, I assume that we live in a global society. The educated population is increasingly exposed to competing and evolving images of democratic values, and population mobility is likely to increase even more rapidly than it has during the rural-urban migrations of the last century. Culture and mobility interact in important ways that will affect our future discussions about education and democracy (Dalpino 2001).

Three perspectives on democracy

I limit my discussion to three alternative democratic theories that frequently underlie policy discussions about democratic values and education in the USA. These are: *democracy as individual opportunity* (liberal democracy), *democracy as social opportunity* (democratic socialism) and *participatory democracy*. These are not the only democratic theories,[2] but I have selected them because each is present, in varying degrees, in educational policies, newspaper commentaries and educational rhetoric in the countries with which I am familiar – e.g. western democracies.

In addition, I will focus on two key questions that are posed by the three theories:

* Whose schools are these? How are ownership and control expressed under different theories?
* How are valued outcomes determined? What are the means of balancing different valued outcomes?

Liberal democracy

Liberal democratic theories suggest that the purpose of society is to benefit the individual in their development. These theories, which underpin the dominant culture in most English-speaking countries, assume a role for public education in ensuring that the polity supports the individual in becoming autonomous and in gaining 'the good life' (Gutman 1995). The role of the state in education is to ensure that the circumstances of the individual child's family (and/or decisions by parents and community members that could harm the child's future) do not prevent access to learning that could benefit the child. In education, political liberalism is based also on Emile Durkheim's (1956) assumption that individual decisions about education need to be balanced against society's need for an educated citizenry. Thus, liberal democratic theory contains a clear tension between societal needs and individual choice (Noddings 1999).

Discussions about liberalism and schooling typically focus on whether schools prepare individuals to take advantage of their rights and fulfil their obligations as citizens. In recent history, this perspective was clearly articulated in a 1940 manifesto by faculty members at Teachers College (Faculty 1940). A response to the growing world crisis, the manifesto outlined the importance of education as a system of meanings underlying democratic principles. The manifesto contains all of the liberal democratic assumptions that provide the tensions that are inherent in liberal democratic theory, including:

- commonality within a diverse population;
- respect for individuality and individual participation within a willingness to abide by majority decisions;
- the rights of minority groups coupled with 'a widespread system of free education' that is largely determined by the majority.

The moral imperative of democracy from this perspective is the combined emphasis on the worth (and responsibility) of each individual in a popular sovereignty that includes strong government.

Democratic socialism

Social democratic theories are prominent in most European countries. Although familiar in English political theory through the enduring influence of Beatrice and Sidney Webb on the Labour Party (Webb and Webb 1920), social democracy is recently defined (somewhat tautologically) as 'progress toward a democratic socialist society' (Esping-Andersen and Kersbergen 1992: 188). The emphasis is on social rights and equality, which need to be balanced against the short-term emphasis on economic or social efficiency. While often identified with a 'welfare state', social democratic principles are present in most countries in movements that emphasise the cohesive presence of groups and stress the importance of redistributing social good – including education – to benefit the working, or otherwise disenfranchised, classes.

Social democratic theories are, perhaps, most prominent in the educational policies of the Scandinavian countries, particularly Sweden. The emphasis on the corporate state as a consensus-driven instrument for social equality is present, but more contested, in other countries, although Christian democrats provide a functional alternative in many settings (Esping-Andersen and Kersbergen 1992). In countries such as the USA, where social democracy is an undercurrent, this perspective is often subsumed under populist or agrarian labels.[3]

The social democratic assumption is that education is a scarce resource and is often inequitably distributed. Wealthy families can purchase the schooling that they want for their children, and do so as a group, through private schooling or their dominance in community settings. A 'resourceful and educated citizenry', on the other hand, is the major constraint against the oligarchy of the privileged (Ramon 1999). Thus, most democratic nations have divided their educational systems into a large 'public sector' (supported by public funds) and a smaller 'private sector' (an option that is supported only by parental/ individual contributions, available only to a small elite).

Participatory democracy

Democratic theories presume participation and ownership, and are based on the Greek ideal of citizenship and the importance of the *agora*, a municipal setting in which citizens congregate to decide important issues (Janowitz 1980). In the USA – arguably the most vocal proponent of this set of values (Heyneman 1995) – democracy is still viewed as most profoundly realised in the New England 'town meeting', in which all adult residents participate and vote on key issues, including educational policies. Under this conception, schools 'belong' to an identified local community that is responsible for determining purpose and process. The central problem is that participation becomes increasingly abstract as size increases, and progressively more opposed by regional, national or even global interests in education (Spring 1996). In educational practice, this often means that participatory democracy becomes reduced to 'parent participation', or the right and obligation of adults to be active in the education of their own children – hardly what Aristotle had in mind.

Participatory democracy values local diversity and responsiveness to the community. Policies in many countries support the right of parents and other groups to diverge from the community at large and develop publicly funded schools that meet specific local needs – policies that are at odds with most liberal and social democratic assumptions (Strike 1999). 'Quasi-independent schools' are, by definition, value-based, whether those values are religious or pedagogic, and are an increasing presence in most established democratic states (O'Reilly 1999). Even relatively homogeneous countries, such as Sweden, have enacted legislation supporting alternatives to the previously unassailable 'common school'. In some countries this means that citizen groups can petition to develop semi-autonomous schools that address the values of a specific group, and may include recognition of the rights of parents to educate their children outside of an authorised school.

The challenge is that participatory democracy at the local level presupposes reasonable congruence of national values. The US legal tradition of locally organised schools is called into question in historic cases such as civil rights and special education legislation, where other principles override local values. In the Netherlands, there is a current debate over the possibility that parent chartered and publicly funded Islamic schools may be teaching values that undermine democracy as it is defined in Holland (Veilignheidsdienst 2002). This tension is particularly apparent around the question of minority rights (an increasing concern in most modern democracies), because of the global shifts in population. This is no longer just a 'North American problem'. Immigrant groups pose a particular challenge in many countries that were previously relatively uniform in belief systems and values (Singh 1999).

Who owns the schools? Perspectives from democratic theory

I have hinted that the three theories lead to very different assumptions and questions about how schools should be organised. The liberal and social democratic perspectives assume that schooling is largely a government responsibility. Societies may differ on the issue of where ownership is vested – national government, state or provincial government, or local community – but the ownership issues and responsibilities are clear. Schools do not 'belong' to teachers, parents or students: they belong to socially constituted and elected units. Participatory theory leads to another position – namely that schools should reflect the needs and desires of those who are active members: parents, teachers and students.

Liberal and social democracy

In liberal and social democratic theories, citizen power is limited to competing for recognition and voice at the ballot box. Historically, liberalism and social democratic theories have advocated common schools while tolerating a small private school sector. The belief that a moderately uniform system can protect both individuals and the state is difficult to sustain in increasingly pluralistic countries: groups that seek recognition and autonomy increasingly contest bureaucratic control by the majority. In Australia and Canada, for example, there are recognised public spheres that incorporate elements of non-state ownership combined with public funding: public (Protestant) and 'private' (Catholic) (Lawton 1986; Potts 1999). In Canada, there are also recognised ownership issues related to language (Francophone vs. English). Pluralistic pressures are also increasing in countries such as France, where the homogeneous common school was an unquestioned value until recently (Fowler 1992). The separation of Church and state or the identification of state schools with a single religion is diminishing, even in the USA.

Turning over control to a particular group of parents in a particular setting remains more controversial. The debates over parent-initiated schools are currently playing out in countries as diverse as the USA and Sweden, both of which have authorised quasi-autonomous 'charter schools' in the last decade. Controversy over the clash between national and local values is also embodied in a recent case in Italy, in which a teacher in a school with a predominantly Islamic immigrant population was criticised for removing crucifixes from her classroom (Hennenberger 2001).[4] Thus, there are increasing 'bottom-up' pressures to accommodate local preferences, through more liberal 'opting out' policies that are reinforced by both right and left parties.

Participatory democracy

Size is the enemy of participatory democracy. As nation states grow in size and complexity, professional politicians and national agendas supersede local control in education (Smith and Meier 1994). At the same time, however, there is a press for site-based management and accountability in a number of countries, such as England, Australia, the USA and the Netherlands, which is also viewed as a way of encouraging participation and responsibility at a municipal or school level (Achilles 1994; Louis 1998).

Current advocates for more participation are sometimes allied with the privatisation movement, arguing that local control is more efficient and effective, an empirical debate that will not be addressed here (see Smith and Meier 1994). But participatory *democratic* theory is more closely allied with industrial democracy, which argues that those who work in them should govern workplaces or have immediate interests in them,[5] and with John Dewey's notions of democracy as 'reappropriated daily at the local level, where it is refashioned in cooperative activities . . . expressing still-existing communal bonds' (Antonio 1989: 739).[6] This raises the issue of how parents, students, community members and professional employees relate to one another. Who must petition for permission to make changes? Who can overrule presumptive actions? Answers to these questions determine the issue of who is the owner and who is the participant. 'Site-based management', which confers greater authority over educational decisions to people who work in and with an individual school, has extended this discussion but has not confronted the underlying ownership question (Riley 1998). However, subjecting delegated ownership to close monitoring of either means or results does not feel like genuine devolution.[7] This may account for the bottom-up pressure for full or partial funding for quasi-independent 'charter' schools. The underlying assumption is that democracy at the local level fails to provide the flexibility and policy direction that would permit schools to meet the needs of particular groups of parents and students.

Two other issues further confound the discussion of participation in educational reform: minority rights and student rights (see Chapter 5 and Chapter 6). Both are volatile issues, although the former is currently more salient in the public eye.

Minority rights and democratic participation

Religion provides a traditional base for discussing the importance of values in local schools, but discussions around participatory democracy are increasingly disrupted by the volatile issue of racism – cloaked in the more neutral term of 'cultural pluralism' (Singh 1999). Local control at the level of school and community has often translated into hegemonic control by vested (e.g. white, politically powerful) school board members (Barnes 1979). Opposition to more devolved control of schools is, according to minority group leaders, based on the assumption that 'black people aren't capable of controlling their own destinies' (Young 1969: 289).

> The potential inconsistency between advocating minority rights and participatory democracy was illuminated by the 1968 Ocean Hill–Brownsville dispute in New York City, in which black power advocates attacked the professional control of teachers and administrators over school management, curriculum and teaching. The facts are less important than the principles, which involved a confrontation over control between two sets of legitimate owners (Fainstein and Fainstein 1976). On the one hand, participatory democracy requires active neighbourhood influence over the operation of public institutions and the reflection of minority interests in local affairs (Fainstein and Fainstein 1976). On the other hand, there is the competing interest of industrial democracy in which expertise based on democratic principles has a role in determining policy outcomes (Furman and Starrett 2002). The major issue in

this case was community, and the size of the governmental unit that should condition ownership. While it is easy to say that New York City is too big to be truly participatory, it proved more difficult to determine what the precise nature of participation and ownership should be.

The issue of minority ownership is fresh on the current educational reform agenda. In the USA we have seen the (contentious) rise of charter schools and other 'schools of choice' whose curricula reflect the desires and aspirations of particular communities (Meier 1997), but which are viewed by some as 'anti-democratic' deviations from the liberal principle of common schools (Wrage 1992). These schools, and the right to choose them, receive vocal political support from minority constituencies, while dominant groups express concerns about racial segregation. In the Netherlands, the increasing number of schools based on Islamic educational principles is consistent with the constitutional support for value-based schools, but inconsistent with other democratic principles (Veilignheidsdienst 2002).

Does democratic ownership include students?

The community control issue masks a narrower but equally import-ant issue, one rarely discussed in democratic theory, but which is prominent in some proposed educational reforms: that is, the role of students as workers and owners. Whether schools, as organisations, have a responsibility for democratic organisation involving students is rarely discussed except in academic circles.[8] A number of scholars have argued that the absence of democratic principles in the organisa-tion of schools is a major impediment to school reform (White 1986; Sarason 1986). Although Sarason's work is frequently cited in the USA, it has not typically raised the question of student empowerment in public discussions of school organisation, which has been left to critical theorists (McLaren 1989; Freire 1994). Student empowerment is largely regarded as a pedagogical rather than an organisational issue, except by educational philosophers such as White, and is limited in practice to private and/or alternative schools that enrol a small number of students.

Efforts to create participatory democracies in schools are often transient, because they lack broad consensus around underlying organisational principles (Oakes *et al.* 2000). In thinking about this issue, I am deeply influenced by a large, public high school that I studied more than a decade ago (unpublished). A largely minority school on the outskirts of a large, impoverished urban centre, the school's principal and staff determined that they wanted something other than a control-oriented strategy toward the disciplinary issues that were beginning to arise. The civic structure of the school was reorganised to give students – all students, including those usually labelled as troublemakers – responsibility for maintaining civil and social support. The details of how this was done are not relevant. The important point is that the effort was successful, low cost – and temporary. Although students, teachers and administrators made presentations to other schools that encountered disciplinary and/or racial problems about the efficacy of their ideas, there was limited diffusion. When the principal retired, the newly recruited school administrator eliminated the real empowerment of students over discipline and social support. Although faculty members were distraught, neither the school board nor the community questioned the changes. In sum, this case reveals the flimsy organisational base on which most efforts to devolve responsibility and decision making authority rest.[9]

Determining the outcomes of schooling: democratic theories and their values

All democracies seek to prepare children to 'attain the equipment in knowledge and attitude required to carry on our democratic way of life' (Faculty 1940: 8). This consensus breaks down, however, over what our democratic way of life will be, and opens up a wide area of questions around hidden and overt power over what is taught and how schools are judged as meeting public needs. Liberal theories argue that individuals 'vote with their feet' and that every responsible government unit gets the schools that they deserve and are willing to support – again, participation at the ballot box. Because it is in society's interests to protect and prepare the young, democracy in action will sort out the appropriate goals. Social democracy argues that there is a difference between protecting the young and protecting vulnerable classes of students (low income, rural or minority). Without state control over the allocation of resources to promote equal outcomes, the critical democratic goal of equalising opportunity cannot be achieved. Participatory democratic theory suggests that the goal is an ephemeral ideal that can only be embodied by allowing the immediate participants in the educational project to make these assessments. While the state should ensure that schools meet minimal standards that protect children from abuse or exploitation, parents, students and teachers should choose what is to be taught, when and how. Participatory democracy accepts that school organisation and its outcomes will vary – and that this is beneficial because it enhances democratic participation.

Liberal democracy

Liberal democracy now demands an international standard that may be increasingly at odds with local participation in determining what knowledge and outcomes of schooling are valued. Thus, the liberal democratic stance on how educational standards are determined cannot be disengaged from assumptions about economic development. The global economy, which presumes a wide and rapid spread of ideas and political movements without regard to local or national boundaries, will determine what people need to know (MacBeath *et al.* 1996). At their core, liberal theories accept the notion that education should prepare individuals to assume lifelong learning goals that support multiple careers in varied locations. Face-to-face and representative democracy will be replaced with other means of engaging highly educated and personally flexible individuals in the polity, just as the twentieth-century industrial division of labour created new forms of social solidarity that replaced governance by guild and family (Durkheim 1947).

The challenge of the global community often pre-empts liberal support of local control. This trend is particularly evident in the English-speaking countries, where, until recently, university entrance requirements had more impact on secondary school curricula than state school-leaving standards.[10] Emphasis on standards, however, is tempered by the continuing value placed on individual choice and freedom (Labaree 2000).

Persistent inconsistency between national economic aspirations and freedom in education has been particularly evident in policy discussions in the Netherlands over the last 20 years. Like most countries, Dutch schools do not demonstrate equality of outcomes for their students, nor are Dutch liberal democrats satisfied that students are prepared to maintain the significant position in the international economy that the Dutch have come to expect over many centuries. In spite of a strong mixture of government schools (30 per cent) and (publicly funded) private schools (70 per cent), the 1960s and 1970s saw increasing centralised control over school policy. In the mid-1980s, a liberal philosophy was introduced, which argued that schools – at least the non-government schools – should be responsible *only for outcomes*. This resulted in a decrease in financial and personnel regulations, but an increase in standardised testing and inspection to determine whether schools were doing their best to produce acceptable results. The shift was hailed by the liberal party (VVD) as a means of freeing individual schools to make local adaptations that would be liberating and, at the same time, able to achieve more equal results.[11] In sum, individual families in the Netherlands still have the right to choose their children's school and its religious beliefs, but have less and less control over the socially approved outcomes of education.

This observation can be generalised beyond the Netherlands. In the European Union (EU), for example, the issue of Spanish children being less prepared to take their place in the international economy than are rural Danish children is apparently of greater concern than educational principles and pedagogies remaining Spanish or Danish. Similarly, the US public is increasingly less tolerant of traditional, regional and state-by-state variations in schooling attainment.

Social democracy

Social democratic theory has always advocated common schools with common standards. Ideally the education system should guarantee equality of educational outcomes, irrespective of differences in family or residential location. Persistent class- or race-based gaps in achievement are regarded as morally wrong, and evidence that schools are not operating effectively. Scandinavian countries, for example, have long prided themselves on the relatively small size of class-based attainment differences, and have viewed this as a justification for policies that, for example, ensure uniformity in the quality of teachers, programmes and facilities between schools.

Social democracy is, however, under attack as a result of increasing social diversity and the ascendance of liberal parties in many countries. Developed countries with growing immigrant populations and substantial variations in both class and group values encounter demands for more, not less, variability. These trends undermine the former emphasis on the common schools – for example, publicly funded schools with a common purpose.

It came as a shock to many that Afro-American parents in the USA are more likely to endorse public subsidies for private schools and charter schools than the population as a whole. Their assumption is that government schools are failing to meet their particular needs, and that private approaches are worth trying. Research in the USA suggests that the demand from minority parents for distinctive schools does not stem from holding different hopes for their children (Farkas and Johnson 1998). Rather, they have differing beliefs about the kind of education that will support successful citizenship and participation in their communities.

As an example, Minneapolis has had a public choice system for nearly four decades.[12] The first form of public choice, initiated to promote desegregation, involved the founding of schools with alternative pedagogic philosophies. From the beginning, Afro-American parents were typically more interested in the schools that promoted stricter standards of student behaviour, fewer choices for students and direct instruction. They explicitly valued the educational outcome of learning how to analyse and work within structure. Middle-class, white parents were the most avid consumers of 'open school' models, which were loosely based on John Dewey's notion of democratic education and student control. These parents, in other words, valued the educational outcome of developing student autonomy. In order to balance the racial integration goals with family choice goals, one awkward compromise has been to establish schools-within-schools that pair middle-class choices (French immersion) with racially based choices (a Native American focus). The resulting schools are racially balanced at the school, but not at the classroom, level.[13]

In sum, social democratic principles, well established in some countries for decades, are experiencing a challenge from globalisation and the erosion of the belief on the part of minorities and economically disadvantaged groups that a common school with standard outcomes is serving their needs.

Participatory democracy

Whitney Young (1969), a strong advocate for community control, argued that the allocation of power to local agencies gives the community 'the clout needed to develop an educational structure and process that will be responsive to the needs of the local community and *accountable to it for its success*' (p. 286, emphasis added). Even in an increasingly global economy, most people respond to changes not by moving, but by modifying their aspirations or careers to fit their desire to stay rooted in their community. In an odd way, participatory theorists and business interests are aligned, arguing that students should be prepared to become productive in their local setting. The notion of productive citizenship is related to local circumstances, and the importance of participation in determining outcomes is also reflected in contemporary educational theories. Constructivism argues that student learning is based on individual and shared experience, whether in the classroom or the community (Prawat and Peterson 2000). Progressive curriculum theory has long argued that student outcomes are grounded in experiences connected to their immediate environment. Participatory theorists would argue, for example, that better learning of history will occur if students research the backgrounds of former slaves buried in a local cemetery than if they are exposed to an excellent curriculum on the Holocaust (Toole 2000). And who is better able to make that judgement than those who live in the community and participate in the school?

However, in most countries local participation in determining educational outcomes may be verbally espoused, but is also regarded as a threat to progress in creating equality of opportunity or global standards. The tension between participation and equality of 'inputs' is evidenced in most countries by the increasing effort to provide full government funding for virtually all schools – and to hold them to similar, if not identical, standards of services.

Colliding expectations and a research agenda

The argument of this chapter is that the notion of democratic schools is extremely problematic, but that we cannot afford to overlook it or brush it off if we are to make sense of current issues of educational reform and schooling. What does it mean to establish a school organisation in which student outcomes are evidence of democratic principles? After reviewing the literature in this area, I see many competing claims, but few efforts to forge a coherent set of principles that would tie school organisation to its larger sociopolitical context.

We sometimes confuse different definitions of democratic schools with national educational systems. Americans look askance at Germany, where students and their parents 'choose' different models of education with different educational possibilities at a young age, and are even more disturbed by the class-segregated quasi-public systems in England and Australia. Germans, in contrast, view American education, which promises (but does not deliver) equal opportunity outcomes at the school level, as demonstrably undemocratic, while the English and Australians can clearly point to US class segregation, which transfers into differential course offerings and expectations by school location in the USA. The same can be said for positive efforts to transfer ideas about how to organise schools across national boundaries, without paying attention to the subtleties of how democracy and participation are embedded in policy, both within and across countries (Louis and Versloot 1996).

How much difference in school-based opportunity and organisation is tolerable in a democracy? The answer varies, depending on democratic theory. Participatory theory suggests that, assuming an educated population, variable cognitive outcomes on tests and measures of post-secondary attendance are a necessary byproduct of freedom for parents and students to choose what is important to them (with some safeguards).[14] Liberal democracy and social democracy both argue for the importance of equitable outcomes. Liberal democracy tends to focus on equality of opportunity; social democracy argues for the need to address social inequities in the educational process. Liberal democracy judges equity on the basis of inputs (do all students have the same opportunity to develop as productive social individuals?); social democracy focuses more on the outputs (do students from disadvantaged backgrounds do well in further education and occupational attainment?).

If we look at Table 3.1, in which I have summarised some of the underlying value tensions among the three theories, it should become clear that differences in policy discussions between countries are less significant than the fact that all the value questions are present in every country (albeit in different guises).

The table summarises some of the unresolved issues that sociologists, organisational theorists and leadership scholars need to consider if they are to make sure that their research addresses the larger question of how schools fit into the twenty-first century. We are not required to provide empirical research about democratic values, but we do need to address how and to what degree the perspectives that we take in our research are explicit and interpretable in light of ongoing debates about democracy, ownership of schools and educational outcomes.

The issues that I have raised, although theoretical, are documented only by reference to easily available articles that deal directly with the intersection of democracy and school organisation. They ignore questions that can only be answered through case studies of the use of language around particular instances of school reform and policy, and around the controversies that accompany visible assessment of the effectiveness of schools.

My comments also ignore the degree to which we need to give more attention to the relationship between schools as organisations and larger social structures in our preparation of school administrators. Clearly we have recognised the need because we include attention to

Table 3.1 Hypothesised value and organisational tensions in democratic theories

	Liberal democracy	Social democracy	Participatory democracy
Who owns?	Designated authority	Nation state	Local and small-scale community
What outcomes?	Locally determined, with some oversight by nation state	Nationally determined by majority consensus	Locally determined
Political value issues	Balance of control between local and higher authorities	What are the rights of divergent groups?	Size and composition of community
Social value issues	How to ensure equal opportunity	How to balance individual and social goods	How to maintain social cohesiveness in the larger society
Organisational value issues	How to prevent hegemonic control of powerful groups – e.g. elected officials, unions and administrators	Balance between individual choice and equality of outcomes	Balance of professional versus citizen input; creating a participatory organisation

financing, policy and equity in our programmes. I question, however, whether we encourage our students to think deeply about how different conceptions of democratic values impinge on schools other than as forces that constrain administrative action. If administrators don't understand (or at least appreciate) the differences, working with diverse and complex communities will become increasingly challenging.

We are in the midst of enormous social changes that will affect all institutions, but schools and universities in particular: the shifts that we encounter daily place more emphasis than ever on knowledge and learning. As nations confront global changes, they will continue to ask serious questions about whether their values will sustain them (or be sustained) through the maelstrom. Over the last decade, at least in the USA, we have encountered value-based challenges to the status quo, ranging from communitarian critiques of our liberal democratic traditions, to pessimistic analyses of the decline of civil society, to demands to teach 'core values' in all classrooms (to name only a few). These expressions of concern represent a challenge to all public organisations, not just to schools (Klay 1998), but they are challenges to which we, as educators, school effectiveness researchers and improvers, must respond.

Notes

1 I gratefully acknowledge the extensive comments of Daniel Bratton on several earlier drafts of this chapter.
2 As Murphy's (2000) work suggests, a single country may develop many disputed models of governance. Governance debates constitute one visible expression of largely unarticulated democratic theories.
3 In Minnesota and the surrounding Canadian provinces, for example, the agrarian-socialist movement is rooted in the political assumptions of social democracy.
4 In the USA, the collision of state and local agendas has played out in the legal arena more than the legislative. Much of this has resided in the question of 'minority rights' and religion, because of constitutional issues (Gutman 1995). The debates are, however, largely superficial from a sociological perspective, because both deny 'parents the right, even in the name of religious freedom, to prevent their children from being taught toleration . . . along with mutual respect and deliberation among people who pursue many different ways of life' (p. 576). In other words, the protection of state interests in educating democratic citizens outweighs parent, student and teacher preferences. Charter schools, which are locally 'owned' but publicly funded, must establish that the 'different values' that they embody are non-exclusionary and solely educational.
5 There is a small but persistent examination of worker ownership as a socialist phenomenon (Pateman 1970) but this has rarely been applied to education (Keith 1996). In addition, there is an increased press in western democracies for more participation by recipients of services, making pro-grammes more democratic (Hills 1998). Critical theorists (e.g. Habermas 1996) focus on related concepts such as 'action in the emancipatory inter-est'. The latter refers to group reflection and action that lead to freedom from ideology and action in the interests of social justice.
6 Dewey was not naive, and did not believe that the local basis of demo-cracy was reflected in national-level dialogue (Antonio 1989).
7 This observation ignores the implementation studies that suggest that site-based management often shifts responsibility from one administrative level to another, rather than actually empowering teachers or parents (Leithwood and Menzies 1998).
8 Habermas, for example, assumes that emancipatory action will involve students, teachers, administrators and parents, but does not fully explain how ideology generates the main constraint against altering the power

relations between adults and children that are present in all societies (Lakomski 1987).

9 A recent search of ERIC (Educational Retrieval and Information Centre) revealed only a handful of articles that make the empirical case for student democracy at the school level.

10 It is incontrovertible that no English-speaking country (with the possible exception of Australia) has succeeded in establishing consensus around the desired outcomes of education, and how schools should be organised to achieve those outcomes. Increased government control over curriculum and accountability for student learning has revealed (and made more contentious) differences in what students know and are able to do within the formally agreed curriculum. In the USA, in particular, there is increased public debate around issues of equity – at least if we interpret discussions around the obvious differences in the performance of minority and lower-class populations as evidence of inequity that are framed under the notion that all students deserve an equal right to the 'opportunity to learn' but that outcomes are a consequence of individual effort and choice.

11 The policies continue to acknowledge controversial differences in curriculum across schools that permit, for example, fundamentalist Protestant schools to exclude the teaching of evolution as science, and the separation of girls and boys in Islamic schools.

12 For readers unfamiliar with the political geography of the USA, Minneapolis is situated in the part of the country that was most influenced by the agrarian socialist movement, and still retains approaches to most policies that are strongly influenced by social democratic principles.

13 The evolution of charter schools in the Twin Cities area has continued to mirror these differences in choice.

14 Variability in organisation is not always associated with variability in outputs. In the USA, which has limited opportunities for opting out of the public school system, 'home schooling' students who have no organised public school experience do as well on standardised achievement tests and in post-secondary education as students who have been through the public school system, and are socially as adept as their public school peers. This has been, of course, a shock to liberal democrat advocates of public schooling, which is based on the assumption that parental preferences, unchecked, will lead to inequitable outcomes and constraints on mutual tolerance (Gutman 1995).

References

Achilles, C. (1994) Democracy and site-based administration: the impact on education, *NASSP Bulletin*, 78(558): 12–21.

Antonio, R. (1989) The normative foundations of emancipatory theory: evolutionary versus pragmatic perspectives, *American Journal of Sociology*, 94(4): 721–48.

Barnes, W.J. (1979) Developing a culturally pluralistic perspective: a community involvement task, *Journal of Negro Education*, 48(3): 419–30.

Dalpino, C. (2001) Does globalization promote democracy? An early assessment, *The Brookings Review*, 19(4): 45–8.

Durkheim, E. (1947) *The Division of Labor in Society*. Glencoe, IL: The Free Press.

Durkheim, E. (1956) *Education and Sociology*. Glencoe, IL: The Free Press.

Esping-Andersen, G. and Kersbergen, K.v. (1992) Contemporary research on social democracy, *Annual Review of Sociology*, 18: 187–208.

Faculty, T.C. (1940) Democracy and education in the current crisis, *Teachers College Record*, 42(2): 99–115.

Fainstein, N. and Fainstein, S. (1976) The future of community control, *American Political Science Review*, 70(3): 905–23.

Farkas, S. and Johnson, J. (1998) Looking at the schools: public agenda asks African American and white parents about their aspirations and fears, *American Educator*, 22: 30–3, 38–9.

Finkelstein, B. (1984) Education and the retreat from democracy in the United States, 1979–1986 *Teachers College Record*, 86(2): 275–82.

Firestone, W. and Louis, K.S. (2000) Schools as cultures, in J. Murphy and K.S. Louis (eds) *Handbook of Research on Educational Administration*, 2nd edn, pp. 297–322. San Francisco: Jossey Bass.

Fowler, F. (1992) School choice policy in France: success and limitations, *Educational Policy*, 6(4): 429–43.

Freire, P. (1994) *Pedagogy of Hope: Reliving Pedagogy of the Oppressed*, trans R. Barr. New York: Continuum.

Furman, G. and Starrett, R. (2002) Leadership for democratic community, in J. Murphy (ed.) *The Educational Leadership Challenge: Redefining Leadership for the 21st Century*, vol. 101. Chicago: University of Chicago Press.

Gutman, A. (1995) Civic education and social diversity, *Ethics*, 105(3): 557–79.

Habermas, J. (1996) *Between Facts and Norms: Contributions to a Discourse Theory of Law and Democracy*. Cambridge, MA: MIT Press.

Hennenberger, M. (2001) Reading Italy's signs of the cross, *New York Times*, 11 November: 4.

Heyneman, S. (1995) America's most precious export, *American School Board Journal*, 182(3): 22–6.

Hills, D. (1998) Engaging new social movements, *Human Relations*, 51(12): 1457–76.

Janowitz, M. (1980) Observations on the sociology of citizenship: obligations and rights, *Social Forces*, 59(1): 1–24.

Keith, N. (1996) A critical perspective on teacher participation in urban schools, *Educational Administration Quarterly*, 32(1): 45–79.

Klay, W.E. (1998) Trends and paradoxes affecting the present and future environments of public organizations, *Public Administration Quarterly*, 22(2): 133–60.

Labaree, D. (2000) Resisting educational standards, *Phi Delta Kappan*, 82(1): 28–33.

Lakomski, G. (1987) Critical theory and educational administration, *Journal of Educational Administration*, 25(1): 85–100.

Lawton, S. (1986) A study of choice in education: separate schools in Ontario, *Journal of Educational Finance*, 12(1): 36–48.

Leithwood, K. and Menzies, T. (1998) A review of research concerning the implementation of site-based management, *School Effectiveness and School Improvement*, 9(3): 233–85.

Louis, K.S. (1998) A light feeling of chaos: educational reform and policy in the United States, *Daedalus*, 127(4): 13–40.

Louis, K.S. and Versloot, B. (1996) High standards and cultural diversity: cautionary tales of comparative research, *Educational Evaluation and Policy Analysis*, 18(3): 253–61.

MacBeath, J., Moos, L. and Riley, K. (1996) Leadership in a changing world, in K. Leithwood, J. Chapman, D. Corson, P. Hallinger and A. Hart (eds) *International Handbook of Educational Leadership and Administration*, pp. 223–50. Dordrecht: Kluwer.

McLaren, P. (1989) *Life in schools: Introduction to Critical Pedagogy in the Foundations of Education*. New York: Longman.

Meier, D. (1997) Can the odds be changed? *Educational Policy*, 11(2): 194–208.

Murphy, J. (2000) Governing America's schools: the shifting playing field, *Teachers College Record*, 102(2): 57–84.

Noddings, N. (1999) Renewing democracy in schools, *Phi Delta Kappan*, 80(8): 579–83.

O'Reilly, R. (1999) The public philosophy and charter schools: Alberta's charter schools, *International Journal of Educational Reform*, 8(4): 342–51.

Oakes, J., Quartz, K.H., Ryan, S. and Lipton, M. (2000) *Becoming Good American Schools: The Struggle for Civic Virtue in Educational Reform*. San Francisco: Jossey Bass.

Pateman, C. (1970) *Participation and Democratic Theory*. Cambridge: Cambridge University Press.

Potts, A. (1999) Public and private schooling in Australia: some historical considerations, *Phi Delta Kappan*, 81(3): 342–5.

Prawat, R.S. and Peterson, P. (2000) Social constructivist views of learning, in J. Murphy and K.S. Louis (eds) *Handbook of Research on Educational Administration*, 2nd edn. San Francisco: Jossey Bass.

Ramon, L. (1999) Preparing students for democratic citizenship: codes of conduct in Victoria's 'Schools of the Future', *Educational Research and Evaluation*, 5(1): 41–61.

Riley, K. (1998) *Whose School is it Anyway?* London: Falmer Press.

Sarason, S.B. (1986) *The Culture of the School and the Problem of Change*. Boston, MA: Allyn and Bacon.

Singh, B. (1999) Responses of liberal democratic societies to claims from ethnic minorities to community rights, *Educational Studies*, 25(2): 187–204.

Smith, K.B. and Meier, K.J. (1994) Politics, bureaucrats, and schools, *Public Administration Review*, 54(6): 551–65.

Spring, J. (1996) Democracy and public schooling, *International Journal of Social Education*, 11(1): 48–58.

Strike, K. (1999) Can schools be communities? The tension between shared values and inclusion, *Educational Administration Quarterly*, 35(1): 46–70.

Toole, J.C. (2000) Implementing service-learning in K-8 schools: Challenging the learning grammar and the organizational grammar of 'real school'. Paper presented at the AREA conference, New Orleans, 20 April.

Veilignheidsdienst, B. (2002) *De democratische rechtsorde en islamitisch onderwijs (Democratic Principles and Islamic Schools)*. The Hague: Binnenlandse Veiligheidsdienst (Office of Internal Security).

Webb, S. and Webb, B. (1920) *A Constitution for the Socialist Commonwealth of Great Britain*. London: Longmans, Green & Co.

White, P. (1986) Self-respect, self-esteem, and the school: a democratic perspective on authority, *Teachers College Record*, 88(1): 95–106.

Wrage, W. (1992) School choice and the comprehensive ideal, *Journal of Curriculum and Supervision*, 8(1): 28–42.

Young, W.M. (1969) Minorities and community control of schools, *Journal of Negro Education*, 38(3): 285–90.

4 Learning democracy by sharing power

The student role in effectiveness and improvement

Mats Ekholm

Introduction

The theme of this chapter is democratic learning and its relationship to school effectiveness and improvement. There are several ways to interpret democratic learning. One is to see the learning that happens in schools as a preparation for life in future situations within a democratic society, so requiring a particular form of knowledge to be built up at school. Another way is to see essential learning as something distributed among different groups. In this view, learning to be democratic means that there is an equal distribution of important subgroups in a school population: the two genders, different ethnic groups or different socioeconomic groups. A third way to interpret this is to look at the rights of students and find out how these are treated by teachers and school principals. To be democratic, the learning that takes place at school needs to be based on real power sharing between the learner and the teacher. The views that children and young people hold need to be accorded respect by staff and learning seen as something that students own and have essential influence over.

The first viewpoint can be asserted in a more limited way and in a more elaborated one. The more limited view sees it as enough that students learn the content of the curriculum. If students are well educated in the various subjects chosen by school decision makers, it is assumed that they will be well equipped to participate in the future democracy. There are many examples of studies of school effectiveness which rest on that premise. They limit their measurement to the results of knowledge tests in traditional school subjects. This immediately distorts the outcome of schools and says nothing about the readiness of the students to participate in democratic procedures. Nor do such measures tell us how well pupils are able to solve problems of an applied mathematical kind or how well they might use written language in real life situations. Recent developments within the field of school evaluation and educational research do, however, offer some hope. The International IEA (International Education Assessment) Civic Education Study, for instance, helps different states to compare how well the students have succeeded in picking up what might be useful to them in a democratic society.

When you look back it is interesting to note what little has been done on the measurement of such longer-term outcomes of schooling. Yet, the idea of using schools as places to train young people to become members of a democratic society goes back more than a hundred years in some western states. We might be entitled to expect many more studies on how the democratic mind is influenced by schooling. But we simply do not find a rich literature on how schools have promoted democratic aims.

There are, however, books written about democratic learning. Some have their origin in discussions held a century ago arising out of interesting experiments that were going on in the fairly new democracies that existed at that time. Practical experiments were made to use schools as places for model learning. Almost everything inside these schools was designed to serve the purpose of simulating democracy so as to help young people to learn from their day-to-day experience. Some of these early experimental schools were found in the USA. One of the most well-known of these was the George Junior Republic School in Freeville, NY. Its programme was widely disseminated throughout the USA at the beginning of the twentieth century. In this school, students elected their own president, who actually shared some of the power of the government of the school with the principal. The whole environment of that school was a kind of simulation of the real democracy of the USA at that time and the students not only participated in decision making, but also held different posts of responsibility within the school.

A little later, during the 1920s, there were schools in the early Soviet Union that used the same dynamics to help students participate in the young democracy that, it was believed, would succeed the old regime. In these schools, designed by A.S. Makarenko, young people who had suffered from the many years of war and the succeeding civil war were rehabilitated into modern life. Makarenko used internal democracy among his students to get them to set norms that promoted more civilised forms of behaviour. The schools had student councils and many of the students held responsible positions, helping them to understand democracy through authentic experiences. The students in these schools did not only learn together, but they also had to earn their living by playing an active role in the surrounding society, as the war economy had left very little to the schools for basic things such as food and firewood.

Perhaps the most interesting of the school experiments that occurred around the beginning of the twentieth century was the laboratory school that Dewey managed in Chicago. In this school the ideas of the French philosophers were practised for the first time on a full school-wide scale. Here students learned democracy by sharing power over the decisions about what should be learned and how the learning should proceed.

There have been many followers of these early experimental schools in many countries. In Sweden we started to follow the ideas of Dewey from the 1920s onwards as a basic pedagogical ideal that fitted well with contemporary thinking about how students could be given more respect in schools. From the late 1940s, with the fresh memory of the evils of dictatorships in mind, Sweden chose to use its schools and the education given there as a kind of vaccine against fascism. Since then we have built in several components in everyday school life to make students used to democracy by participating in it from the earliest years. In Swedish schools, students and their teachers hold class councils, usually once a week. Students elect representatives to school councils which discuss important matters in the school about once a month. The climate of the schools is such that students discuss their learning with one another and with their teachers and address other relevant issues. The effects of this are seen in students' responses to international surveys on discipline, such as in the recent Organisation for Economic Cooperation and Development (OECD) Programme for International Student Assessment (PISA) (2001) in which Swedish schools share the lowest rankings on indiscipline along with schools in other North European countries which also promote student voice in their schools. The students in schools in these countries report that they have a good rapport with their teachers and feel free to express their views.

Longitudinal studies of internal democracy in schools

Although at system level in Sweden there have been concentrated efforts to make schools good places for learning knowledge and skills useful in the democratic society of the future, these skills usually take second place to academic achievement. It is commonplace for the training in democratic skills to be set aside in favour of academic goals. Therefore, the pace of development in schools to improve the quality of democratic learning is not very high. The case of nine Swedish schools that I have studied over 25 years (Ekholm and Kull 1996) illustrates what I mean. We carried out a survey in 1969 with teachers and students of Grade 8 in nine comprehensive schools, when the students were 15 years old, asking them how often they participated in decision making relating to 11 specific issues. They were asked to estimate the frequency on a four-point scale, running from 'always' via 'rather often' and 'not very often' to 'very seldom or never'. We went back to the same nine schools in 1979 and again in 1994 and asked the same questions to see what changes had occurred.

The items covered decisions taken about things like school dances, where to go on study visits, the content of discipline rules in the school and in the school yard, how commonrooms should be furnished, choosing the contents of homework assignments and knowledge tests, fundraising and the food in the school canteen. There were also items about decisions taken regarding the state of the restrooms and the rules about smoking at school. The overall results of these 11 items, represented by the percentage of students saying that they had participated in decision making 'always or rather often', are shown in Figure 4.1.

The effort that the Swedish school system made to create lively internal democracies in schools which would stimulate students to

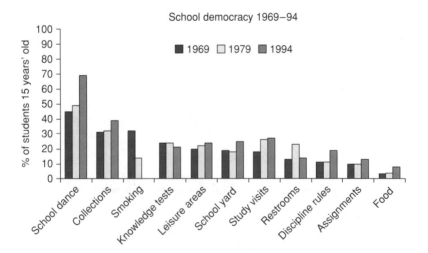

Figure 4.1 Estimations made by students of how often they participated in decision making at school in terms of 11 different issues (% of students N 1969 = 1141, 1979 = 1206, 1994 = 1036)

participate in their society was not evident in the data. When the results of the nine schools are combined, they show a substantial percentage of students having a say in only 4 of the 11 items. The two items that show the largest increase – school dances and collections – are two aspects of school life that occur less often. Other everyday phenomena, such as the content of homework assignments and knowledge tests, do not show a similar increase. In one area students have lost all power – that is, to decide on rules about smoking at school, since the government has completely forbidden smoking in schools. One conclusion of this study is the need to widen the scope of participation in order to improve school quality.

The variations among the nine schools are small, as can be seen in Figure 4.2, which gives an index of students' perceptions of school democracy. The index has a lowest value at 11 and a highest value at 44. There are only two schools that have improved their internal student democracy during the 25-year period, which is not too complimentary for the schools or for the Swedish school system. In order to improve this inner quality of a school there is a need for systematic work, building on and evaluating outcomes on democratic skills as well as academic attainment. It is also apparent from this study that schools need to use existing knowledge about school improvement if they are to achieve the aims which the state prescribes.

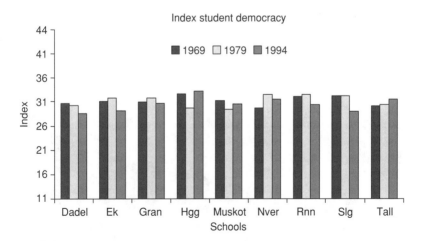

Figure 4.2 Estimations made by students on three occasions (1969, 1979 and 1994) of how often they have participated in decision making at school in terms of 11 different issues (% of students in nine different comprehensive schools in Sweden)

The study of the nine schools over 25 years is the longest study of one school cohort that I know. Within a year another longitudinal Swedish study will be finished following 35 schools by means of interviews 20 years on from the start of the study. Blossing and Lindvall (2002) will report on that study soon and will then be able to show if there are happier outcomes for democratic training in Sweden. We are also preparing a follow-up study in 2003 of a national evaluation that was originally conducted in 1992, giving an 11-year longitudinal study of over 100 Swedish schools which comprised the sample of the original study.

Meanwhile we are able to reflect some of the trends in this area by using data from a broader attitude survey that was repeated in 1994, 1997 and 2000. As we do not have access to data from the same schools in each of these years, we have to rely on three different random samples of Swedish students aged 14 to 18. Students were asked to judge to what degree they felt that they had participated in decision making in seven areas of school life. These covered what books were used, the quality of the food, school rules, homework assignments, changes in the school environment, what to learn and also how to learn at school. The results of this study are presented in Figure 4.3.

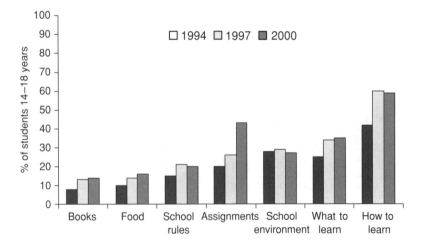

Figure 4.3 14–18-year-old students' judgement of to what degree they have participated in decision making in seven areas (% of students who say that they have participated to a 'large' or 'rather large' degree).

This study reveals a change in schools during the latter years, showing an increasing number believing they do have influence over important issues such as what they will learn in class as well as in homework assignments. The reliability of the survey is high, suggesting that the long period of discussion within Swedish teacher unions and between the *kommuns* that employ teachers, seems to have borne fruit. This may be explained by a shift in the attitude of the teacher unions in the late 1990s. Instead of resisting changes in schools, the unions declared that they were prepared to take the lead in improvement work. Salary scales have now been reconstructed, with differential salaries now the norm and in many schools teachers being paid more if they contribute to their school's improvement.

Better use of the knowledge on school effectiveness and school improvement

If we wish our schools to be places where young people enjoy the kind of experiences which will promote democratic participation in society, we will need to apply the best of what we know from effectiveness and improvement research. To help schools to be places of democratic learning we will need to draw on findings from school improvement, but this faces two major challenges. The first is dissemination to users and the second is utilisation by users.

Knowledge about school culture and the development of schools grew steadily during the twentieth century. Early sociological works such as that by Waller (1932) as well as those on the social psychology of teaching have been updated several times. Mort and Cornell (1941), who studied the pace of American school reform during the 1930s, laid down useful paths for others to follow. In the 1950s and 1960s Gordon (1957) and Coleman (1961), contributed to our understanding of the dynamic interrelationships among students in order to explain school effectiveness. Also in the 1960s Miles (1964) contested Mort's and Cornell's view that innovation in schools is a slow process in the inner workings of propounding a view of the healthy organisation (Miles 1965) while Sugarman (1969) elaborated on the school as a social system. Both these texts have stimulated later researchers in their understanding of the inner lives of schools. Bocoock (1972) and Schlecty (1976) provided useful summaries of sociological and social psychological research on schools during the 1970s.

British empirical work on schools, social life and transformation has grown from the early work of Hargreaves (1967, 1972) to more recent work building on this theoretical groundwork combined with theories of management of change (Hargreaves and Hopkins 1991). Stenhouse (1977) highlighted the importance of seeing school and school change from a teacher's point of view. In Scandinavian countries Ekholm (1971) studied the inner lives of schools and contributed to the understanding of the social development of students (Ekholm 1976).

In the 1980s, cooperation among different countries in terms of their approaches to school improvement was stimulated by the OECD. Based on Dutch initiatives, more than a dozen volumes of condensed knowledge on school improvement were produced. They covered themes such as useful school improvement knowledge (Velzen *et al.* 1985), what is known about the long-term effects of school improvement efforts (Miles *et al.* 1987), dissemination of successful practices (Berg *et al.* 1989), the use of school-based review as a tool for change (Bollen and Hopkins 1987), how school improvement can be supported (Seashore Louis and Loucks-Horsley 1989) and the role of school leaders in school improvement (Gielen *et al.* 1987). This cooperation brought American and European school improvement researchers together and an intense exchange of ideas took place.

During the early 1990s new overviews of the knowledge on school improvement were published. Fullan (1991), assisted by Stiegelbauer, wrote extensively on the meaning of educational change, showing that despite the volume of knowledge that exists there is no commensurate evidence of improvement in schools. His thesis is strongly supported by the longitudinal Swedish studies of 35 schools carried out during the period from 1980 to 1985 (Ekholm 1987) and of 9 schools during the period from 1969 to 1994 (Ekholm and Kull 1996). In both of these longitudinal studies schools appear to change very little despite strong external pressures to improve their internal procedures and despite strong support for that process.

Fullan (1991) is not alone in reviewing our imminent state of knowledge about school improvement. Murphy and Hallinger (1993), Guskey and Huberman (1995) and Hargreaves *et al.* (1998) have also made substantive contributions to our knowledge of the processes of school improvement. Fullan ends his overview of the field with some advice on how this growing knowledge might be better used. He proposes replacing an older, poorly functioning paradigm of school improvement with a new one based on 'six pillars'.

He argues for a change in thinking from a negative to a positive politic, requiring that any individual who wants something good to happen to work continually to shape and pursue what is valuable. He further proposes that people who desire positive change need to be encouraged to seek alternative solutions instead of monolithic ones. He supports this argument with reference to successful school improvement investing in some form of partnership between schools and school districts. He counsels schools to work in alliance with others and also to change the thinking from an 'if only' to an 'if I/we' perspective, in other words rather than looking for why things are difficult, schools should adopt a 'can do' perspective drawing on the rich knowledge that already exists about the change process.

We know many things about that process but it is a complex and fruitful field, and not one that should be oversimplified. Fullan especially draws attention to the fact that improvement work needs long-term conditions of change if it is to be sustained. He concludes that we must shift from development in schools based on single innovations to a broader institutional development. He identifies the problem of change and stability in schools and how this can generate more innovations than is possible to manage in sequence, leading to projects 'completed' but without vitality. The lesson from this is to create an infrastructure for ongoing organisational improvement rather than implement a large number of isolated innovations.

These lessons parallel the perspectives that Murphy and Hallinger (1993) present in their analysis of school restructuring research. They argue for a retrospective mapping of prospective change through the eyes of students, focusing on the improvement process itself. They also recommend systematic work, combined with school-specific approaches to improvement, reminding us of the extent to which schools need external support in order to achieve better solutions. In addition to some structural developments they also see cross-fertilisation between schools as an important component of the development process as well as for the professional development of teachers.

Smylie (1995) describes how schools might be redesigned to facilitate learning among teachers. He points to inbuilt qualities of schools such as teacher collaboration, shared power and authority between teachers and educational authorities. Along with egalitarianism among teachers he advocates variations, challenge, autonomy and choice in teachers' work. Smylie pays attention to the need for schools to have access to multiple sources of information for learning and external referents which help schools to receive a flow of feedback on their efforts. He also makes a plea for schools to accept teacher learning as a part of the definition of teacher work, so that the learning of teachers can be an integrated part of the daily working life of the school.

In some studies of schools that have developed practices that improved the quality of students' learning, these elements of a futuristic knowledge base have been put to use. For instance, Huberman and Miles (1984), in their close look at innovation processes in 12 schools, presented evidence for several of the six conclusions that Fullan drew from his literature overview. In two Scandinavian cross-national studies (Vasström 1985; Ekholm 1986, 1990), where 15 improvement-oriented schools were followed over five years, several aspects of the knowledge basis for lasting improvements were identified. For instance, the importance of cross-fertilisation between schools, the acceptance of improvement processes as complex ones, taking a broad approach to change and stimulating learning among teachers as part of the daily work are some of the components of improvement that were supported by the studies. These findings are further supported in two other cross-national studies (Dalin *et al.* 1994; Hameyer *et al.* 1995). In the first of these, changes in 31 school sites in three developing countries were analysed and in the second study the history of 15 schools in four industrialised countries that had succeeded in institutionalising activity-based practices in their inner working lives were analysed. Additional evidence comes from a study conducted in rural Pakistan of 32 schools with differing degrees of success with their students (Farah *et al.* 1996), as well as from the studies by Liyanage and Perera (1995), Wijesundera (2000) and Perera (2000) of improvement in disadvantaged schools in Sri Lanka.

The knowledge that exists today about how school improvement can be effective is rich but full of subtle differences and nuances. The problem is, as Tydén (1995) argues, that there is considerable evidence that school people ignore knowledge that is produced by researchers, one reason being that researchers create their knowledge from a different perspective than that used by practitioners. Another reason seems to be that there are difficulties in getting school people to critically assess, re-examine and adapt the knowledge to their own immediate context.

During the 1990s, researchers tried to formulate further knowledge theses to prevent a repetition of earlier shortcomings. It is important that these theses are understood and disseminated if we wish to create a more stable and reliable knowledge base about school improvement. I doubt, though, that the formulation of these theses will be of real help to those who are trying to improve school performance. This is because, during the last few decades, very little has been done to use what is known about the inner lives of schools, about the factors that create effective schools, about the mechanisms behind successful innovative work in schools and about the institutionalisation processes in schools. Or, it might be better to describe the use of this widening knowledge as restricted to the small number of people scattered widely around the world who have grasped and used the knowledge. Unless that knowledge penetrates the day-to-day knowledge that permeates teaching and pre-service training programmes, change is unlikely to occur.

In the late 1970s the focus shifted and the terms 'school effectiveness' and 'school improvement' were used to refer to two different areas covering adjacent parts of the knowledge territory. School effectiveness immediately appealed to the conservative politicians that were dominant in the USA and England. The political leaders in these two countries changed the rules of the game for researchers. It became difficult to secure state funding for studies of the egalitarian and grass-root democratic strategies of school change that had developed through the 1960s and 1970s (e.g. Schmuck *et al.* 1975). The rational restructuring of schools was more attractive, with a hope of quick results in slow working social organisations. The term to describe the knowledge field in the USA became 'restructuring', whereas in Europe other territorial labels were retained. As Creemers and Reezigt (1997) show however, there have been tendencies to link school effectiveness thinking with school improvement from the mid-1980s onward.

Practical use of school effectiveness and school improvement knowledge in Sweden

The real test of the quality of school improvement will be seen when the less interested and less enthusiastic users begin to engage with that knowledge. But before reaching a situation where a broader use of what we know about improvement is apparent we need to face the problems of disseminating knowledge and helping it to be seen as important and relevant. Knowledge about school improvement seems to be most easily adopted by people who already share the same perspective of schools as the knowledge producers. One such group is school leaders, who share the view with most researchers in the field of schools as locally managed organisations. In Sweden, new school leaders have, since the middle of 1970, been through national programmes that exposed them to literature, ideas and activities based on school improvement knowledge (Ekholm 1992). These participants have started to use the ideas, but one important lesson emerging from this long-lasting and ongoing field experiment in knowledge dissemination is that the knowledge is still difficult to apply day to day. In an effort to apply knowledge, school leaders frequently report difficulties in getting teachers to share the same perspective. Their primary interest is in the classroom and they do not share the commitment of school leaders to the creation of new improvement infrastructures.

At the national level in Sweden we are attempting to broaden the use of school effectiveness and improvement knowledge led by the organisation that I am the head of, Skolverket (in English, the National Agency for Education). The agency has three main tasks. One is to legally control what is happening in preschool, primary school, secondary school and adult education in the country. The second task is to carry out evaluations in the educational system and a third task is to stimulate improvement work in different parts of that system. The central purpose of these initiatives is to promote democratic processes, but to be effective the impulse for change has to be at the level of local organisations – that is, in the schools themselves.

To make the achievement of Swedish schools visible, an internet-based information system called SIRIS has been developed. Information about the 5100 comprehensive schools and 650 secondary schools in the country can be found here. On one of the sub-web pages of skolverket.se it is possible for anyone to access the SIRIS system. Inside the website of SIRIS, you can find presentations of results from national tests, summations of students' grades, the annual quality report which schools are expected to deliver, national quality reviews and some basic information about the specific schools such as size, costs, composition of students by sex, ethnic background and the educational level of the parents. The information is aggregated and presented at school level. It is possible for the user of the system to find the above-mentioned information for any individual school and to make comparisons between different groups of schools. If, for instance, you want to find out how your local school compares to other schools that are similar, it is possible to make those comparisons and compare results over time.

Within SIRIS we have chosen to present the results of Grade 9 comprehensive school students, estimated by the average sum of their marks, but controlling for the relative effect of three background characteristics of the students. We recalculated the results of the schools using regression analysis, taking into account established research that has shown that the mix of students with different socio-economic and national backgrounds together with the gender mix explains a large proportion of the statistical variance. We present the calculated residual effect and use it as a measurement of the relative achievement of the school. Of course this measurement does not reflect the quality of the single school, but makes it more possible for the school to understand the value of its own achievements. While we do not use this information to rank schools, some newspapers have taken the opportunity to make comparisons. After some debate in the press a more relaxed and informal level of discussion seems to have developed.

We have great hopes of helping people to get used to this kind of open presentation of school results to feed into their own internal discussions about the quality of the work at the school and to discuss the distribution of different resources for improvement. So far we seem to have succeeded at least in one aspect of getting this corpus of knowledge on school effectiveness and school improvement accepted. Less confusion seems to lie between the use of the general concept of 'school' as a system and 'school' as a site where learning takes place with its own unique qualities that differ from other sites.

As the information available in SIRIS is accessible to anyone, there is also analytical help on the internet. When you have chosen the information that you want to use, you are offered help via the web. Online texts describe how to interpret the results that you have chosen to look at. You can also find out when the information was collected, by whom it was collected and what groups were examined. Documents that describe important aims and guidelines are accessible too, as well as links to relevant national-level evaluation reports.

Over the last four years an interesting method has been employed to enrich the national school evaluation strategy in Sweden. As well as the arsenal of knowledge tests and statistics about school performance, 'connoisseurs' from different areas of the educational system have conducted quality reviews in schools. The government decides annually on two or three areas of concern on which the Skolverket, with help from its connoisseurs, reports. Such reviews play an important role in the ongoing debate about those specific areas and give policy makers and the public a better understanding of what quality means in each area and the nature of the problems that affect it. Examples of issues covered during latter years include: school management, the training of reading skills, sex education, contracts for tender in education and the practice of marking. This year we are concentrating on the way in which schools inform others about their work, the use of time in schools and how they sustain motivation for learning. The report presented to the government about the situation concludes with recommendations for improvement for different actors in the system, such as schools and *kommuns*. It is recognised that this information may not be representative of the whole country, as only 20–40 *kommuns* are typically included in the annual sample.

The reviewed themes are scrutinised by officials from Skolverket in cooperation with experts in those fields.

All schools and *kommuns* in Sweden have been requested to present annual quality reports for several years, in which school results and practices are discussed in relation to national guidelines. The state, represented by Skolverket, not only publishes annual quality reports on the internet, but also becomes involved in improvement dialogues with the *kommuns*. It will take Skolverket staff five years to hold such dialogues with all 289 *kommuns* in the country.

In addition to the quality report of the *kommun* and its schools, the Skolverket has put more information on the table to stimulate discussion. During a series of meetings the *kommun* and Skolverket discuss the quality of the local school system and the two parties try to find consensus on a shared understanding of any shortcomings. This shared insight into local problems helps to develop creative discussions about possible solutions. The dialogue ends in an agreement between the state and the *kommun* about improvement, with both parties committed to taking action over a period of approximately two years. Most of these actions consist of new patterns of work among teachers and school managers, but may also include participation in networks with other schools in the country and engaging with research in relevant fields. Skolverket can provide funds to support the *kommuns* in their agreed programmes of improvement strategies. Dialogues maintained between the *kommuns* and Skolverket, that are based on local quality reports and information from the national level, are evaluated by external bodies. A review will be presented in 2003. Olsson (2002) describes this work in greater detail.

Conclusions about democratic learning

If schools are to be living examples of participative democracies that we can learn from, old habits, structures and strategies will need to be re-examined. Long and well-established traditions and working patterns do not make democratic learning easy. Schools have been designed to be places were teaching is at a premium, but *teaching* can eat into a student's time for important *learning*. This is especially true for democratic learning which is a matter of experience. To be able to learn, democracy students need to be able to raise important questions, to participate in decision making, to take responsibility for the decisions they take and to participate in the evaluation of the whole process. All these steps in a democratic process take time and all are in competition with the teachers' priorities for the use of that time – 'covering' the curriculum. However, to support young people to learn democracy, more time in schools needs to be used for experiential learning and less time given to traditional teaching.

We need to break a long tradition of how schools' aims are formulated and communicated. These aims need to be constructed in such a way that not only school staff can understand but students as well. If schools are not simply to pretend at internal democracy, but practice it for real, students will need, together with their teachers, to have a share of understanding of the challenges that face their schools. If either party does not know the rules of the game they are expected to play, it makes it difficult for any real cooperation to take place, or for realisation of school goals to be achieved. Time needs to be made for students and teachers to discuss the meaning of democracy in their schools, and for the distribution of power between participating parties. This implies teachers accepting less privileges and power for themselves and recognising that, if they are unwilling to accept that, students for their part will be prevented from carrying out responsibilities that make democratic experiential learning possible.

Democracy is based on tensions and conflicts, and living with tension and resolving conflict is an integral part of the democratic process and integral to school improvement. So, schools cannot turn a blind eye to tensions but should learn to understand and work with internal conflicts. Democracy needs to be seen not simply as a broad social concept, but also as a basic attitude that permeates everyday life and is practised in a variety of forms. As it touches fundamental values and beliefs, families need to be a part of the dialogue so that students are helped to cope with the sometimes conflicting demands of home and school. It is equally important to invite politicians to schools, so that students can experience the 'logic' of political life in the world outside school. Encounters with politicians are especially important when students have tried to influence local decision making about issues important to them (e.g. local traffic conditions or school resources) and are waiting to see the results of their actions.

To help students to learn democratically it is surely better to allow the same teachers to follow their students for an extended period of time, since democracy requires a long-term perspective. Democratic learning systems where teachers meet their students for one year and then do not see them again for the rest of their schooling are less effective than the strategy used in Denmark, where the same teacher may follow students through the school for nine years in sequence.

For democratic learning to become a reality, teachers themselves need to learn more about democracy, democratic attitudes and

110   *Mats Ekholm*

democratic decision making. In-service training opportunities need to be used to experiment with decision-making structures, where teachers become acquainted with different ways in which students may be encouraged to raise questions, prepare for decision making and reach those decisions satisfactorily.

When we have used in-service teacher training for this purpose in Sweden, we have been struck by the fact that so many teachers are not accustomed to taking advantage of the full repertoire of opportunities available to them in involving their students in the democratic process.

The democratisation of schooling is not for lack of knowledge, nor for want of successful models of school and classroom practice. The literature on school improvement is large and growing daily. The successful translation of its principles into schools in Sweden and other countries suggests that the distribution of power in schools can be changed and students can be leaders in making their schools more effective places for democratic learning.

References

Berg, R.v.d., Hameyer, U. and Stokking, K. (1989) *Dissemination Reconsidered: Demands from Implementation.* Leuven: OECD-ISIP, ACCO.

Block, P. (1987) *The Empowered Manager.* San Fransisco: Jossey Bass.

Blossing, U. and Lindvall, K. (2002) Skolors förbättringskultur 1980–2001. Karlstad: University of Karlstad.

Bocoock, S. (1972) *An Introduction to the Sociology of Learning.* Boston, MA: Houghton Mifflin.

Bollen, R. and Hopkins, D. (eds) (1987) *School-based Review: Towards a Paxis.* Leuven: OECD-ISIP, ACCO.

Coleman, J.S. (1961) *The Adolescent Society: The Social Life of the Teenager and its Impact on Education.* New York: The Free Press.

Creemers, P.M. and Reezigt, G.J. (1997) School effectiveness and school improvement: sustaining links, *School Effectiveness and School Improvement,* 8(4): 396–429.

Dalin, P. with Ayono, T., Biazen, A., Dibaba, B., Jahan, M., Miles, M.B. and Rojas, C. (1994) *How Schools Improve: An International Report.* London: Cassell.

Ekholm, M. (1971) *Skolans anda och miljö.* (*School's Atmosphere and Milieu*) Gothenburg: Institute of Education, University of Gothenburg.

Ekholm, M. (1976) *Social Development in Schools: Summary and Excerpts.* Gothenburg: Institute of Education, University of Gothenburg.

Ekholm, M. (1986) *Fjorton nordiska skolor ser på sin egen utveckling. Sammanfattning av skolornas slutrapporter i samarbetsprojektet Organisationsutveckling i skolan. (Fourteen Nordic Schools Looking at their Development)* Köpenhamn: Nordisk Ministerråd.

Ekholm, M. (1987) School reforms and local response: an evaluation of school reviews in 35 school management areas in Sweden 1980–1985, *Compare*, 17(2): 107–18.

Ekholm, M. (1990) *Utvecklingsarbete och elevstöd i vidaregående skolor i Norden.* (*Development Works and Support to Students in Further Education in the Nordic Countries*) Nord. Köpenhamn.

Ekholm, M. (1992) Evaluating the impact of comprehensive school leadership development in Sweden, *Education and Urban Society*, 24(3): 365–85.

Ekholm, M. and Kull, M. (1996) School climate and educational change: stability and change in nine Swedish schools, *EERA Bulletin.* 2(2): 3–11.

Farah, I. with Mehmood, T., Amna, A., Jaffar, R., Ashams, F., Iqbal, P., Khanam, S., Shah, Z. and Gul-Mastoi, N. (1996) *Roads to Success: Self-Sustaining Primary School Change in Rural Pakistan.* Oslo: IMTEC and the Institute of Education at the Aga Kahn University, Karachi.

Fullan, M. with Stiegelbauer, S. (1991) *The New Meaning of Educational Change.* New York: Teachers College Press.

Gielen, K., Glatter, R., Hord, S. and Stegö N.E. (eds) (1987) *The Role of the School Leader in School Improvement.* Leuven: OECD-ISIP, ACCO.

Gordon, W.C. (1957) *The Social System of the High School: A Study of the Sociology of Adolescence.* Glencoe, IL: The Free Press.

Guskey, T.R. and Huberman, M. (eds) (1995) *Professional Development in Education: New Paradigms and Practices.* New York: Teachers College Press.

Hameyer, U., Akker, v.d. J., Anderson, R.D. and Ekholm, M. (1995) *Portraits of Productive Schools: An International Study of Institutionalising Activity-Based Practices in Elementary Science.* Albany, NY: State University of New York Press.

Hargreaves, D.H. (1967) *Social Relations in a Secondary School.* London: Routledge & Kegan Paul.

Hargreaves, D.H. (1972) *Interpersonal Relations and Education.* London: Routledge & Kegan Paul.

Hargreaves, D.H. and Hopkins, D. (1991) *The Empowered School: The Management and Practice of Development Planning.* London: Cassell.

Hargreaves, A., Lieberman, A., Fullan, M. and Hopkins, D. (eds) (1998) *International Handbook of Educational Change.* Dordrecht: Kluwer.

Huberman, M. and Miles, M.B. (1984) *Innovation Up Close: How School Improvement Works.* New York: Plenum Press.

Liyanage, S. and Perera, W.J. (1995) Improving the institutional development capacity of disadvantaged schools: A Sri Lankan experience. Paper presented at the ICSEI Conference, Leeuwarden, the Netherlands, 3–6 January.

Miles, M.B. (ed.)(1964) *Innovation in Education.* New York: Teachers College Press.

Miles, M.B. (1965) Planned change and organizational health: figure and ground, in R.O. Carlsson *et al.* (eds) *Change Processes in the Public Schools.* Eugene, OR: University of Oregon, CASEA.

Miles, M.B., Ekholm, M. and och Vandenberghe, R. (1987) *Lasting School Improvement: Exploring the Process of Institutionalisation.* Leuven: OECD-ISIP, ACCO.

Mort, P.R. and Cornell, F.G. (1941) *American Schools in Transition.* New York: Teachers College Bureau of Publications.

Murphy, J. and Hallinger, P. (1993) *Restructuring Schooling: Learning From Ongoing Efforts.* Newbury Park, CA: Corwin Press.

Olsson, G. (2002) Introducing reciprocity and mutuality in school improvement processes. Paper presented at the ICSEI conference on Democratic Learning, Copenhagen, January.

Perera, W. (2000) *The Co-relation Between Student Achievement and School Factors in 43 Sri Lankan Schools.* Maharagama, Sri Lanka: National Institute of Education.

Schlecty, P.C. (1976) *Teaching and Social Behavior: Toward an Organizational Theory of Instruction.* Boston, MA: Allyn & Bacon.

Schmuck, R.A., Murray, D., Smith, M.A., Schwartz, M. and Runkel, M. (1975) *Consultation for Innovative Schools: OD for Multiunit Structure.* Eugene, OR: Center for Educational Policy and Management, College of Education, University of Oregon.

Seashore Louis, K. and Loucks-Horsley, S. (eds) (1989) *Supporting School Improvement: A Comparative Perspective.* Leuven: OECD-ISIP, ACCO.

Smylie, M.A. (1995) Teacher learning in the workplace: implications for school reform, in T.R. Guskey and M. Huberman (eds) *Professional Development in Education: New Paradigms and Practices.* New York: Teachers College Press.

Stenhouse, L. (1977) *Curriculum Research and Development.* London: Open University.

Sugarman, B. (1969) The school as a social system, *Moral Education,* 1(2): 15–32.

Tydén, T. (ed.) (1995) *When School Meets Science.* Stockholm: Stockholm Institute of Education Press.

Vasström, U. (ed.) (1985) *Nordiska skolor i utveckling – utvecklingsarbete vid 14 grundskolor i Norden.* Köpenhamn: Nord.

Velzen, W.G.v., Miles, M.B., Ekholm, M., Hameyer, U. and Robin, D. (1985) *Making School Improvement Work: A Conceptual Guide to Practice.* Leuven: OECD-ISIP, ACCO.

Wijesundera, S. (2000) *School Improvement: An Action-based Case Study Conducted in a Disadvantaged School in Sri Lanka.* Peradeniya, Sri Lanka: Peradeniya University.

Waller, W. (1932) *The Sociology of Teaching.* New York: Wiley.

5 Children's participation in a democratic learning environment

Per Schultz Jørgensen

Introduction

How do children see their own situation, in the school, among friends and in the family? In addressing this question I will draw on the international Health Behaviour of School Children (HBSC) study, in which I am involved as part of the Danish research group. I will also discuss children's rights, informed by my experience as a member of the National Board for Children during the 1990s – and as chairman (commissioner for children) in the period 1998–2001, positions which have considerably influenced my views.

Why is it important to deal with the question of democratic learning? In my view the key concepts are the *open society* and the *formation of character*, but the answers to this question are rooted in a political debate. My premise and point of departure is that democracy – even from a child's viewpoint – is always rooted in questions of power, influence, freedom and rights. When we consider rights as defined by the United Nations (UN) Convention on the Rights of the Child we are required to ask whether this convention can ever be implemented in the school, in the real world?

What does democracy mean from the child's viewpoint? What, for them, is democracy? How do children in Denmark and in other countries of the world consider their situation and their sphere of influence in the classroom? Some answers to these questions are provided by results from the HBSC study – mainly from Denmark, but I will also refer to some comparisons between selected countries.

These results provide the basis for a discussion of the link between democratic learning and the formation of character which I see in terms of well-being, influence and personal growth. The connection is a belief that the inner learning environment – mind, thoughts and knowledge – is shaped by the pattern in the outer learning environment

– the climate in the classroom, social relationships and the degree to which you are able to exercise personal influence. It is therefore unreasonable to expect a mature formation of character in the inner learning environment if we deny children opportunities of influence in the outer learning environment.

Taken together these provide the developing ground for competence – the ability to handle your own life. Being allowed scope to have a say, to be heard, to develop competence in a supportive, democratic, social context, to deal with the expectations that others hold of you – that is formation of character!

Finally, what can we learn from practical school initiatives which take children seriously as active participants? In a way, the conclusion of this chapter comes right at the beginning: if teachers or school leaders want personal development and formation of character to be an essential part of the learning process, then this process must be democratic in nature. This is especially true in the modern world.

But let me start with the political debate!

The political debate

Some believe that there is a contradiction between democracy in the school and learning outcomes among students. They advocate strong teachers and a learning environment based on teacher-oriented methods, and a fixed and prescribed curriculum. They see a clear correspondence between the restoration of traditional teacher authority and solutions to problems such as bullying, lack of discipline and overt behaviour difficulties.

I disagree with this viewpoint and believe that such an argument misses some of the critical issues. I would strongly warn against any return to an old-fashioned teacher role because it is out of step with the times we live in and is inappropriate to the real challenges we are facing. What we need is not only more *dedicated* teachers but more *democratic* teachers. We need teachers who are able to create a learning environment arising from the active participation of children and their progressive development of competence. This difference in opinion is more than a different view of teaching – and it is not new. We have been familiar for many years with the conflict between two views (or two modes) of teaching: teacher-oriented methods versus pupil-oriented methods. And there have been many studies which have tried to evaluate the effectiveness of these two contrasting styles. But this is, in a sense, a superficial viewpoint. The debate is really about deeper paradigms – what a school is *for* and what it is *about*.

This debate is joined by various participants on both sides of the argument. In the USA, for example, Allan Bloom and Jerome Bruner represent contrasting views on school systems and the formation of character in the postmodern world. Allan Bloom wrote his book, *Closing of the American Mind* in 1987 as an attempt to restore tradition in a system broken down by the student revolt and the aftermath of the sputnik crisis. America seemed to be longing for education resting on fixed goals, measures and teacher authority. Jerome Bruner wrote *The Culture of Education* (1996) from a quite different standpoint. He warns us not to go back but to move forward and to face the huge challenges ahead. What we need, he argues, is a school reform movement with a better understanding of where we are heading and a deeper belief in what kind of human beings we want to be – and what we want to see as the outcomes of schooling.

This is a conflict of opinion not only about the teaching process but about the formation of character. Allan Bloom's view is premised on the society of the twentieth century, while Bruner attempts to foresee a social system of the future which places much more responsibility on the shoulders of the single individual. The conflict is essentially a political one because it is about how we define the human being and the kind of society we want to live in. The notion of 'democratic learning' is clearly located, therefore, in a political context.

The political nature of the debate has come to the fore in the last ten years, and has been recently expressed by the French sociologist Pierre Bourdieu (2000) in a lecture he gave in Chicago in December 1999 at a conference on language with the title 'Scholarship and commitment'. We live, he said, in a time of a conservative and neo-liberal revolution that has come into effect after the breakdown of the communist regimes. He continued:

It is conservative, but presents itself as progressive . . . and presents relapses to earlier steps in all fields as reforms and revolutions. Maybe most visible is the effort to roll back the welfare state and the role of the public institutions, and where they do their best to undermine and remove democratic entitlements in the labour market, in the health sector, in the social sector and in education.
(1999: 42)

Strong words and a clear, sharp opinion. Bourdieu's emphasis on the political context is one to bear in mind in any discussion of democratic learning: it will always return to the political question. Treating the democracy of learning as a technical question or as a matter of school organisation is to miss the point. The wider scope of our understanding will be served by keeping the political issue in mind. To be political is also to be social.

The open society

Our understanding of democratic learning also needs to be set in the context of the dramatic changes which have taken place over the last 30 to 40 years. These changes have occurred in all spheres of the society – from technological to cultural and social spheres, from national levels to the most private and personal life spaces, virtually all over the world, and not least in the western world. These changes are associated with key concepts such as the postmodern society, the knowledge society and modernity, all relevant to the fact that we live in a period characterised by a lack of values and common norms and a collapse of the previous traditions linked to social life. We are 'set free', as some would see it; liberated from previous conventions, living in the most individualistic world imaginable.

This modern world has many apologists: Max Weber, Ulrich Beck, Anthony Giddens and Pierre Bourdieu from the sociological field; Norbert Elias, Jürgen Habermas and Kenneth Gergen from a more philosophical viewpoint. However, let me turn to a Norwegian psychiatrist, Finn Skårderud and his 1999 book *Unrest* – which means 'restlessness' (in Danish, *Uro*). It is a description of a kind of journey into modern society and the modern human being. Skårderud explains the modern by saying 'We are set free and enjoy the possibilities. We are set free and suffer from it'. It is an open society and to quote Skårderud:

> Our modern society is intensively explained and covered with words. There is no lack of words. And many of these words are fine analytical concepts – like ambiguity, multiplicity, decentered-ness, vague and fluid, fragmented, fractal, non-linearity and so forth. They all point in the same direction and confirm the old Marx dictum: All that is solid melts into air. Therefore one of the most exact diagnostic concepts to me is complexity – and it has an optimistic flavour. It indicates fragmentation but also, that there is reason in the madness.
>
> (1999: 18)

Children experience this openness in their daily life – from a global television input to the close family circle. The children of today live in what are referred to as 'new family patterns'. In Scandinavia we are able to boast three European and perhaps even worldwide records in this field. We are top of the league in the number of mothers of small children working in the labour force, in the number of children taken care of from the early years in institutions and in the number of children exposed to divorce.

My intention is not to dramatise these figures. They speak for themselves. What I want to emphasise is that the open society exposes to view the day-to-day reality of children's lives. It tells us about the world they have to navigate, to a large extent on their own. In short, this implies a quite different formation of character today as compared to, say, 50 years ago. This is critical to our understanding of the new demands on schools and on the democratic learning process. From now on the task for the school is much greater: it is not simply a question of teaching, but of learning and the formation of character.

We used to talk of conformity to ensure the passing on of our heritage from one generation to the next. Today such conformity would act as a hindrance to real adaptation and growth. Instead it is the responsibility of every individual to establish their own inner stability and self-understanding. But how can this aim be reached in a world of fragmented messages and constant change?

This brings me to the central and most significant challenge of them all – the twin concepts of *choice* and *reflexion*. The individual has to choose, to decide, to act and to understand their own life in a reflexive movement. That means self-centredness but at the same time engenders a profound need for a social context to return to and rely on. The key-words are 'self' and 'social integration' – concepts which have been the cornerstones of modern psychology and sociology for the last century.

But let me again quote our Norwegian psychiatrist Finn Skårderud (1999: 22):

> The psychological man is a reflexive human being – and that means that every one of us constantly must consider who we are going to be, what we shall do and how we shall act. The course of life has always comprised different passages, where the individual has moved from one identity to another. In the traditional society, rites and rituals marked these passages. Our culture is much more transient and it is difficult to maintain stable social identities. Therefore we ourselves have to write our own biographies and create the links between personal and social changes in our life. The body has been drawn into this reflexive project. How shall it be shaped in the best way?

This points to two levels of personal existence: one is the inner world of experience; the other is the outer world of social relations – the private world and the public. To put it in another way: we are reflexive human beings operating in a social context.

Putting these two together we have:

First statement: formation of character
The modern society has placed much more responsibility on the single individual to form its own character – that means the formation of identity, self understanding and social role.

Second statement: participation in learning
If learning should contribute to formation of character then there must be an understandable consistency between the inner and outer learning environment – that means an active participant role in our own learning and in the social environment.

In my view these two statements are clear and logically consistent. You cannot be called upon to find yourself and then be deprived of influence on your own social context. Yet the standard solutions to problems and evidence of social misfits are to return to traditional autocratic ways of dealing with teaching, children and the school environment, despite the obvious logical contradiction for a democratic society and a democratic education system. If we really want children to be able to handle the challenges of the open society, a democratic learning process is a necessary precondition. They must *achieve* ownership, for themselves and in their social context.

Point of departure: the UN Convention on the Rights of the Child

Let me now more directly focus on the question of democracy and the role of the child. The point of departure to me is the UN Convention on the Rights of the Child (1989). This is the most globally accepted of all UN conventions – 179 countries have ratified it. We are still waiting for the USA and Somalia.

The convention covers a variety of rights, and they are all considered to be indivisible and interdependent. The four basic principles are guidelines for implementation, and are:

- non-discrimination (Article 2)
- best interest of the child (Article 3)

- the right to life, survival and development (Article 6)
- the views of the child (Article 12).

It is obvious that Article 12 and the right of children to participate in their own life is crucial when we are talking about democracy. This article states that: 'In accordance with age and maturity
children should be heard and taken seriously in all matters affecting
them including any judicial and administrative matters'. Here we
have a vision and words that all over the world tend to be seen
as revolutionary. The Article advocates that children be subjects in
their own life – not objects belonging to parents or adults. It follows,
therefore, that if we are serious about the convention we must reach
a new understanding of how to draw children into our joint social
environment and help them to become responsible. But is this
possible? Children are, after all, so different, whether according to
age, maturity or culture. How can a 3-year-old possibly be given
influence?

Let me at this point be very specific and refer to a model adapted
from Roger Hart, an American researcher and advocate of children's
rights. The model consists of a ladder or staircase comprising several
steps – from the first one where adults take all the decisions to the
final one where the opposite is true: children decide for themselves.
The 'participation ladder' looks like this:

1 **Adults control:** adults take all the decisions and children are
  informed.
2 **Adults control more gently:** adults take all the decisions, but
  children are informed and explanations are given.
3 **Manipulation:** adults decide what is going to happen and children
  are asked if they agree.
4 **Decoration:** adults decide what is going to happen; children take
  part by singing and dancing!
5 **Symbolic:** adults decide what is going to happen but children are
  involved in matters of lesser importance.
6 **Invitation:** adults invite children to express their opinion but
  decisions are made on adult premises.
7 **Consultation:** adults ask children to express their opinion and
  then make the decision on that basis.
8 **Joint decision:** adults and children contribute to the decision on
  an equal basis.
9 **Children decide with support from adults:** children have the
  initiative in decisions and are supported by adults in their decisions.

10 **Children decide:** children make decisions and adults are only involved if children ask for help.

The important issue in the convention is that children are considered subjects in their own life and this position is reached according to the age and maturity of the child. But what does this mean? What of the 3-year-old? Can they be seen as a subject and given any sense of participation in important matters? Let me tell you about Anna, who is 3.

Anna's parents had sold their house and were going to move to a new one in the neighbourhood. How should they inform Anna? How much should they tell her? And how early? They treated these questions very seriously and debated the information process, eventually telling Anna, 'We are going to move. We shall leave the house and move to a new one and so we shall say goodbye to our old house'. And so they did, with Anna, going around the house, from her own room to the small drawings she had made on the wallpaper to the playground in the garden. Everywhere they said goodbye and 'have a nice time' and thank you. And then they went to the new house, knocked on the door and said, 'Hello, here we are. Good day, how do you do, I am Anna. I am going to live here from now on.' And then they moved with all their belongings.

The next day, when they brought Anna home from the daycare centre and she became aware of the unfamiliar road she said, 'What? Aren't we going home?' And her parents answered – and this is the important point in the story – 'Oh *yes*, certainly we are going home, but don't you remember that we said goodbye to the old house and hello to a new one?' 'Oh yes,' Anna said, 'that's right. I had almost forgotten,' and she sat thinking about it in the car. And she understood something, because she had been involved in the process. When the story is retold in the future, she will be explicitly included as an active participant.

What is democracy in the school?

But what is democracy in the classroom? How far up the ten-step ladder are we able to go when we talk of real life in the school? To be honest, can we even reach Step 6 or Step 7, even when we do our best?

Elementary education has changed dramatically in many schools during the last 15–20 years, no doubt about that – discovery methods, multimedia approaches, emphasis placed on talking, interdisciplinary approaches, team teaching, multiple-track programmes, intergrade grouping, open plan schools where the teachers' role is to encourage, to guide, to clarify and to provide the setting. These are far removed from traditional rows of desks, standard texts and following teachers' precise directions.

But how widespread is this revolution in teaching and learning? To what extent are we able to sustain these advances in today's society? If we address these questions from a social point of view we have to consider democracy as a way of living, as a kind of social conversation or, as expressed by the Danish historian Hal Koch during the Second World War and the occupation of Denmark: 'Democracy is dialogue'. That means that democracy includes attitudes such as involvement, commitment, mutual respect and the search for knowledge. The concept of dialogue not only means an acceptance of differences, but taking departure in these differences and considering them as fruitful for the joint enterprise. Dialogue means '*dia logos*': reason flowing between us, reaching a new common reason which is greater than the individual reason we each possess.

In the classroom and the school system this means democracy understood as culture, as social life and social norms, and this is exactly what Jerome Bruner (1973) is referring to when he asks the question: 'What is the most important subject in the school?' and gives the answer: 'The school itself'. In other words, the social dimension is not an annexe to teaching, it is the very precondition. So, school democracy includes important aspects such as:

- children's well-being
- children's influence
- the question of friends in the school
- the relationship between teacher and pupils
- an absence of bullying.

But in spite of advances in education and teaching during the last few years, how do children see their school environment?

An investigation of school democracy: the HBSC study

How do children themselves experience these big questions about democracy? I can give at least part of an answer by reference to results from the international investigation of 11, 13 and 15-year-olds in more than 30 countries including the Scandinavian countries,

Denmark, many European countries and the USA (Currie *et al.* 2000). It was called the HBSC study and was sponsored by the World Health Organisation (WHO). The most recent results are from 1998, during which a little over 5000 children gave their opinions in a questionnaire. They said things such as:

- school is a nice place
- rules are fair
- school – that is where I belong
- we take part in making rules
- teachers encourage us to express our own views
- teachers show interest in me as a human being.

But the questionnaire revealed a satisfaction rating of only 30–50 per cent: one third were not satisfied while the remainder were neither one nor the other.

I will focus on 11-year-old boys and include only seven countries (see Appendix, p. 127). The three areas I will focus on are:

- 11-year-olds liking school a lot;
- 11-year-olds agree they take part in making rules at school;
- 11-year-olds agree that their teachers are interested in them as persons.

For 'liking school a lot' there were great differences between countries, with Germany at the top and Finland at the bottom. But we have to admit that due to cultural differences this question (as with all the questions) might have been understood differently in the different countries. It is always a little dangerous to make these types of comparison, because you cannot take them at face value.

However, it is obvious that for some questions and in some countries the situation is rather positive: around half of the pupils evaluate the school environment very positively, and belong to a group of children where well-being is part of their daily school life. However, when we look at the question: 'We take part in making rules' this group only comprises one third of the pupils, and the group of students being very positive and strongly agreeing on this question is only about 10 per cent.

I admit that these results can be considered from two sides: the positive one where you conclude that much has been achieved – compared to, for instance, 30 years ago – and the negative one where you conclude that around half of the children were not very satisfied with the school environment, and large groups felt themselves to be outside any kind of influence.

But let me go a little further into the Danish analysis of the study: there are big differences between schools. If we consider the statement 'School is a nice place' we find that in many schools less than half of the pupils felt that this was so. In some schools less than 35 per cent of the pupils belonged to the positive group. How come? The analysis shows a clear connection (i.e. a correlation at a high level) between well-being, fairness, influence and a positive relation to the teacher.

These results lead me to try to construct a preliminary model – or a participant equation – for children's well-being in school:

Students participant role = f (recognition, commitment, influence, social relations, fairness)

This can be shown as a graphic representation of children's well-being (see Appendix, pp. 127–30).

My conclusion is that democracy from a narrow and formal point of view is missing something very important in children's life: their subjective feeling of well-being and their involvement in a process which is a positive contribution to a formation of character. In my view democracy as a way of living is associated with social involvement and social responsibility and a feeling of belonging. Democracy means giving high priority to the social dimensions in the everyday life of a school.

Let me at this point repeat my second statement from page 118: 'If learning should contribute to formation of character then there must be an understandable consistency between the inner and outer learning environment – that means an active participant role in our own learning and in the social environment'. The HBSC study shows that for some of the children in some of the schools this goal seems to be within reach, but for others it is far from likely to be achieved.

What can we do?

If we now face the more difficult question of what to do to change the situation we must admit that we are facing strong barriers to real school democracy. I have already mentioned political conservatism strongly arguing for more weight to be given to traditional subjects and teaching methods. Another barrier is parent organisations. In some parents' minds, school democracy could include the risk of delaying the systematic teaching process and consequently reduce the possibility of a positive outcome for their children. In my view they are wrong in several respects, not least the fact that they equate *education* with *learning*.

We must aim at two different strategies: one is focusing on the social environment and students' subjective feelings of democracy, and the other is focusing on the inner learning environment: a competence-based learning environment. A realistic and practical strategy for improving the social environment for children in schools is to work and argue on different levels, including the political level, the school administration level, teacher education, research and documentation, campaigns for children's rights and initiating practical school experimentation to develop new strategies.

In my view we are right in concluding that schools tend to be more effective in their efforts if their strategy is founded on a bottom-up approach, in contrast to a top-down approach. A good example is a school on the Danish island of Langeland. It is a very small school with not more than about 100 pupils. Here in third grade the pupils, supported by their teacher, decided to set up rules for their social life in the classroom. Among the 13 rules they agreed upon were the following:

- we must only tease in fun;
- if we tease and we are asked to stop then we shall stop immediately;
- we must not beat hard, kick, push or tug someone by the hair;
- we must not tell a lie to the teacher or to each other;
- we shall welcome new classmates and help them;
- we must not interrupt each other;
- we shall remember our home lessons ourselves;
- we must not give each other nicknames;
- we must not take each others' belongings without permission.

After a year of following these self-imposed rules, the climate in the class, particularly in relation to bullying, has greatly improved. This is an excellent example of a strategy devised and implemented by the children *for* the children: they see themselves as subjects; they are made responsible.

There are many pathways to a better social environment and only our imagination sets the limits of concrete experimentation in this area.

A competence-based learning environment

Let me now turn to the inner learning environment and emphasise that this means students dealing with the meaning of the learning process on their own. It is a personal effort to create understanding and we can use many words for this process: wholeness, coherence, perspective, inner motivation, reflective learning, metacognition, personal relevance and generative learning. It is a constructing process, integrating new influences into personal experiences. It is a process of knowing and, to use the title of Jerome Bruner's (1973) book, of learning to go 'beyond the information given'. It is a kind of personal discovery, which takes place anyway, but we should try to enhance the process and make it congruent with the aims of teaching.

It is here that that term 'competence' has come into use, and in my view it is of some relevance when trying to understand personal learning and the practical strategies to take into consideration when we look at the outer learning environment. Competence is a rather old concept in psychology, having been around since the middle of the twentieth century (Jørgensen 2001). Among the numerous contributors to the definition of the concept are Robert White, Albert Bandura, Daniel Stern and Jürgen Habermas. Others could also be mentioned, but the point is that the concept is founded on the anthropology of man, which considers the human being as open to the surrounding world and autonomous in its search for meaning and identity.

I shall not go further into the roots of the concept of competence, but in accordance with these researchers I define the concept as 'a personal qualification of skills'. Competence is not a free-floating ability to handle life or situations, but a *personal* acquisition of skills in a social context.

Competence, then, deals with different levels of reality: the level of practical actions in everyday life; a deep and existential level; and in between a level for reflection on outcomes and strategies, feelings and concerns, connections and losses. My model is a simple one, comprising these three levels:

- skills
- knowledge
- self-understanding.

Skills are what you are taught, the actions you are instructed in. Here you can be measured and tested. How many words do you have at your disposal when you are a 6-year-old? This level can be biological in origin, or social, and here you have the basis for any competence, be it to work, to read or to play the piano.

The next level – the level of knowledge – is one of understanding and consideration, of creating a personal relevance and trying to link this to previous experiences. Here you construct a kind of answer to the questions 'What do I believe? What do I see as my answer to this question?'

The third level, self-understanding, is a private level, a personal level, and is often difficult to put into words. It is the level of personal reflection: how do I manage, how do I cope, how do I succeed? Here you try to answer the question 'Who am I?'

Competence as a personal qualification of skills means that we always try to practise and use our skills in a wider context and with a deeper scope; that we always try to understand both the situation and ourselves and what we are intending to do. If we succeed in this practice and understanding we may talk of competence and ask the following question: how can we improve the conditions for students achieving not only skills but competence? My answer is that there must be an understandable congruence between the outer social and democratic environment, and openness and freedom for students to reflect on their own personal experiences. To qualify in a personal way is to be allowed this reflection and be respected in the process. Social norms must pay respect to this personal process, otherwise we risk creating a 'double bind' situation.

The most important aspect of such a competence-based learning environment is its ability to foster and develop what I will call 'generative learning'. That is to say, becoming involved in a continuous process of discovery and knowledge. It is here that the most important processes of formation of character are founded, because the two kinds of environment are deeply integrated in one another: the inner and personal and the outer and social.

Conclusion

I have tried to lay bare assumptions and to convince. I admit to my double intentions. And looking ahead I ask myself whether I should be optimistic or concerned about the future. I move between both of these feelings and attitudes, sometimes seeing the light at the end of the tunnel, but sometimes suspecting that this is the headlight of a train moving towards me at full speed.

Appendix

Appendix: the HBSC study – selected results

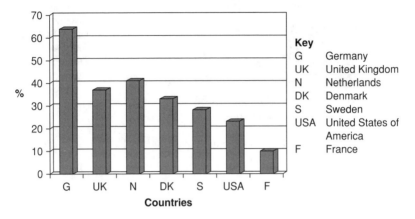

Key
G   Germany
UK   United Kingdom
N   Netherlands
DK   Denmark
S   Sweden
USA United States of
        America
F   France

Liking school a lot: agree (11-year-old boys)

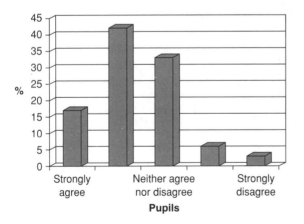

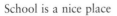

School is a nice place

128 *Per Schultz Jørgensen*

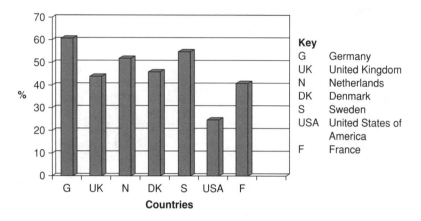

We take part in making rules: agree (11-year-old boys)

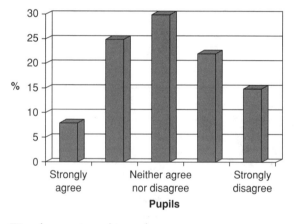

We take part in making rules

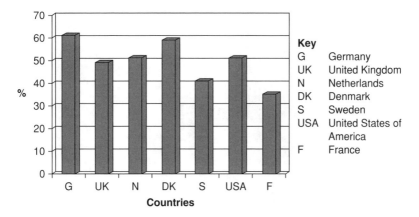

Teachers show interest in me: agree (11-year-old boys)

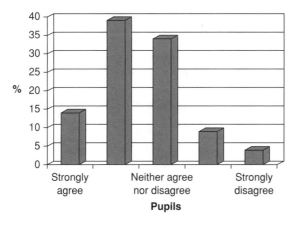

Teachers show interest in me

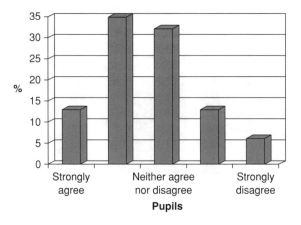

Teachers encourage us express our own view

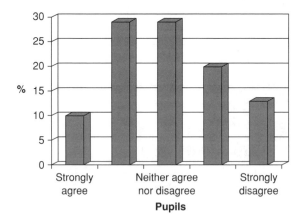

School – that's where I belong

References

Bloom, A. (1987) *Closing of the American Mind: How Higher Education has Failed Democracy and Impoverished the Souls of Today's Students*. New York: Simon & Schuster.

Bourdieu, P. (2000) For a scholarship with commitment. Address to the Modern Language Association in 1999, published in *Profession 2000*, pp. 40–5.

Bruner, J. (1973) *Beyond the Information Given*. New York: Norton.

Bruner, J. (1996) *The Culture of Education*. New York: Harvard University Press.

Currie, C., Hurrelman, K., Settertobulte, W., Smith, R. and Todd, J. (eds) (2000) *Health and Health Behaviour among Young People*, WHO policy series 'Health policy for children and adolescents'. Geneva: World Health Organization.

Jørgensen, P. Schultz (2001) Kompetence – overvejelser over et begreb [Competence reconsidered as a theoretical concept], *Nordisk Psykologi*, 53: 181–208.

Skårderud, F. (1999) *Uro. En rejse i det moderne selv*. København: Tiderne Skifter.

6 The darker side of democracy

A visual approach to democratising teaching and learning

Michael Schratz and
Ulrike Löffler-Anzböck

Using photographs in evaluation

Teaching and learning are embedded in the 'jungle of feelings' of social and physical life in schools. Classrooms are traditionally the places where teaching – and hopefully learning – take place. They are dominated by methods based on the spoken or written word, a cultural and historical relic of academia, whose foundations are built on the written word. School effectiveness research, dominated as it is by quantitative methods and reliant on conventional school parameters, cannot easily accommodate the complexity of visual images and their emotional underpinnings. In the wider canon of educational research comparatively little attention has been paid to the conditions under which education is organised – for example, the physical and emotional connotations of the places kids 'love to hate'.

Conventional methods using language suffer from the fact that the power relationship is too biased in favour of the adults when young people are confronted with verbal argument. This alerts us to the need to seek other ways of looking into the 'inner world' of schools – from the children's perspective, being alert to the potential traps set by language.

If children are given a camera as a research instrument to explore their schools as learning organisations they can find new ways of thinking about social life from a different perspective. They can offer not only the evidence of what one individual sees or documents but an evaluation of their world view, a 'vision' of the relationship between subjects and objects, captured through the medium of visual representation.

Support for the case is made clear in the presentation of this chapter which, in its linear written form fails to capture the impact of the visual presentation. Visual presentation, unlike this chapter, is not linear but multi-faceted and simultaneous. What young people see through the lens of the camera, and what they capture in their photographic frame, demonstrates the 'interconnectedness' between places, rooms and areas, and feelings, emotions and associations. These are things which usually receive little attention in education, and even less in schooling, where teaching is mainly focused on cognitive aspects of the curriculum.

Rob Walker got us interested in using a photographic method in evaluation because, as he put it, 'it touches on the limitations of language, especially language used for descriptive purposes. In using photographs the potential exists, however elusive the achievement, to find ways of thinking about social life that escape the traps set by language' (Walker 1993: 72). His aspiration in using black and white photographs was to find a silent voice for the researcher. For him, looking at photographs creates a tension between the image and the picture, between what one expects to observe and what one actually sees. Therefore, images 'are not just adjuncts to print, but carry heavy cultural traffic on their own account' (p. 91).

These ideas were further developed in Schratz and Walker (1995), who write that there has been a curious neglect of the visual imagination in the social sciences: 'Despite an enormous research literature that argues the contrary, researchers have trusted words (especially their own) as much as they have mistrusted pictures' (p. 72). For them the use of pictures in research raises the continuing question of the relationship between public and private knowledge and the role of research in tracing and transgressing this boundary:

> In social research pictures have the capacity to short circuit the insulation between action and interpretation, between practice and theory, perhaps because they provide a somewhat less sharply sensitive instrument than words and certainly because we treat them less defensively. Our use of language, because it is so close to who we are, is surrounded by layers of defence, by false signals, pre-emptive attack, counteractive responses, imitations, parodies, blinds and double blinds so that most of the time we confuse even (perhaps, especially) ourselves.
>
> (Schratz and Walker 1995: 76)

After having studied more of the theoretical background we were convinced of the power of pictures in research and decided to test how the instrument of photo evaluation would work when put into the hands of pupils. By doing so, we expected them to gain more power in negotiating change with their teachers. We were, therefore, particularly fascinated by the idea of using photo evaluation as a means of democratising teaching and learning. As a result we confronted the pupils with the idea of finding evidence of the places where they feel happy in school and where they would like to bring about change. The answers to these questions are an important aspect in the quality development of a school in which pupils have a significant role to play.

Evaluating places: a photographic approach

How does photo evaluation work?

After experimenting with photo evaluation in several schools we arrived at the following procedure which may be used as a model:

1   Self-selected groups of four or five pupils are formed.
2   Each group discusses the four places in school where everybody in the group feels happy, and four places they all hate.
3   The teams decide which arrangement will best show what they wish to express (e.g. just the place or the people in it).
4   The members of the teams take the photographs according to what has been decided on in 3.
5   When the pictures are developed (immediately with an instamatic camera or print-out of a digital camera), each group has to produce a poster where they arrange the photos and write comments on the pictures to make clear what they like or dislike and why they do so.
6   Each group presents the poster to the rest of the class and, very quickly, they get involved in heated discussions about their situation in the school and about the school system in general. The next step is to organise themselves to change things they consider changeable.

We have learned on several occasions that students are usually not seen as active participants in quality development. Therefore the question is how to find an engaging way of getting them actively involved (and not just as the ones who fill in questionnaires!).

We may think of two different ways of introducing the method to pupils:

- Either start the photo project in a similar way to any other project work without emphasising the evaluation aspect. Perhaps as a consequence nobody will want to change anything, but things do not always turn out as we expect them to. Whether or not the time is 'right' the project may nevertheless turn out to be a 'kick start' for self-evaluation.
- Or start with the project, describing it as one part of the self-evaluation programme that the school has decided to try out (*if* there is such a programme, of course!).

We have tried out both approaches and think it important to take into account the lack of familiarity with self-evaluation, so it might be advisable to get there by a different route, without being explicit about evaluation as the purpose of the project. However, we are sure of this: the more schools use their new found freedoms, the more they will require, and ask for, methods and instruments of evaluation. They will, as a consequence, be in a better position when confronted with public demands for accountability.

Here are some examples of places chosen by the pupils:

- They all choose places where they were allowed to move freely, to feel something, to smell, to do manual work; places like the gymnasium or the art room where the usual predominance of academic work was less to the fore.
- Often they preferred those places in school which symbolise 'the way out' – for instance, windows or the front door of the school. (Comments of one of the groups who had taken a photograph of the front door: 'Wir haben den Ausgang gewählt, weil sich dahinter die Freiheit verbirgt!' ('We have chosen the exit door because freedom lies behind it!') In a similar way, many groups said the small schoolyard was their most cherished place in the whole school.

There are some areas which are seen more ambivalently: An example of ambiguity was the head's office, positively seen because 'you always find a sympathetic ear there' and negatively seen because 'you have to justify yourself there if you have done something wrong'.

Hidden and forbidden places such as the staff room are very appealing on the one hand, because they are taboo places, but on the other hand pupils have said that 'boring lessons come from there' or that this is where punishments come from. Some also commented on the untidiness in the staff room, which made it easier for them to justify their own untidiness in class.

Positive or negative 'appreciation' often depends on the experiences children have had with certain teachers in certain rooms, so for instance the handicraft room gets a minus because members of the group didn't get on with their handicraft teacher.

Another important aspect is offering pupils the chance to break taboos. For example, they can deal explicitly with the toilets, almost the only place in school where they are not supervised, offering opportunities for some creative photos! Isn't it exciting to test how the teacher will react?

What happened during the children's work in groups (Steps 1 to 5)?

As mentioned above, all the decisions concerning the relevant places had already been taken by the teams during Step 2, so we expected them to agree on the most 'fitting' comments within the groups without much further discussion – but we were mistaken. Now they had to look for 'the right expression' to explain the group's choice of photos by the group, and so it was necessary to find consensus in detail on the reasons and to deal with questions of language and communication theory ('Can we find a way to express what we think of our school without being mistaken and misunderstood by the others?'). So they went through the discussion process for a second time, now starting from a more advanced level. In a sense they simply moved through an 'heuristic loop'.

A flavour of the discussions among the pupils is illustrated by what they said while they were writing their comments. One team treated the whole thing from an epistemological point of view and from an aesthetic one as well:

> We must express exactly what we mean. Is it clear what we like and what we hate? You see, everybody looking at our poster must understand what we want to say! Yes, please, listen to me! I do know the right expression now! Oh no, rubbish. Don't. That expression is misleading . . .

Another group was concerned with a question of principle: 'OK, Michael, we know, *you* have had troubles with the handicraft teacher X, and now you want *all* of us to put a negative commentary on the room? Sorry, but *we* haven't had any problems with X and we like to be in this room! What *you* want to write down is not what we think . . .'

In M's team it was all or nothing:

Let's be honest, the only place we should give a plus is the exit, because it's the way out, everything else has to be given a minus, otherwise we are just toadies . . . Not at all, silly child, I love to be in the gym, but you see, I don't care whether it belongs to the school building or not! . . . That's it, it hits the nail on the head. You want us to write positive and negative comments, and what will it look like? Like 'Well, there are nice places there and not so nice places, school is somehow mixed, and so on', and you know that would be a lie, the whole thing is shit!

On the whole we were impressed by how seriously the work was taken by the pupils. The presentation phase turned out to be quite turbulent, each team presenting one poster with photographs and comments as the result of their internal discussions, especially in the case of different opinions as to certain places (and about people connected with these places, of course). Within the groups, emotions ran high from time to time. But on the other hand it was noticeable that many pupils at least made an effort to listen to the arguments of the others and to understand the reasons for their choice, even if they themselves had another point of view. What they had to accept was that the same school was not the same for all of them – different pupils with many different worlds in their minds.

Consequences

The pupils of one class involved in the project meanwhile elected a group of four girls and boys, a team of activists whose job it was now to cope with implementing the various suggestions for change. One outcome was that the pupils wanted their views to 'go public'. In the meantime one of the greatest desires of the class (a cafeteria) had come true, and they had also been able to arrange a discussion with the teacher who had generated the 'minus' for the handicraft room! Besides, something else had changed: teacher-pupil relationships were becoming even closer and more trusting, and as one pupil put it, 'We speak out more freely about what we think of certain things, what we appreciate and what we do not like'.

Teachers' voices

One of the teachers involved in photo evaluation described her experiences:

Photo evaluation was the second project which my colleague and I had carried out together in this class [of 11-year-old children]. Before that we had already developed 'rules of life in the classroom' together with the pupils who seemed to be especially restless and nervous at the beginning of the school year. They wanted to work out rules themselves, and asked us to support them by collecting and moderating their suggestions. This turned out to be successful and so we started another team project, the photo evaluation.

We thought it was a good opportunity to deal with the topic of class community by first placing the new school building at the centre of attention, and we intended to move forward on several levels.

First we preferred working in groups, second we wanted to focus the children's interests on their brand-new school building. To build groups was quite difficult, because how were we to deal with the problem of outsiders in the class? Especially one boy, Markus, who was slightly handicapped and tended to be isolated from the rest of the class. We tried hard to find a solution without simply using teachers' authority, but this was not entirely successful.

It was then that my colleague and I wondered if we had better stop the photo project and turn the topic to 'Markus is handicapped and an outsider in the class', but then we found a 'solution', at least for the immediate present. We allowed Markus to choose the group *he* wanted to join, and so he became a member of one of the two female groups (the class had decided to build groups of girls and groups of boys without any 'gender mix'). This team accepted him as a member, but alas they weren't able to really integrate Markus. He was, of course, aware of the fact that even the girls in 'his' group in the beginning were refusing to work with him, and so he sat down with his back towards the group, pretending to be not at all interested in what was happening around him. His outsider role could not be ignored by the others any longer, so the project was, in a way, an evaluation of the social structure of the class as well.

The Markus issue was never entirely resolved, at least at that time, but for the project as a whole the teacher's conclusion was that:

It was a great pleasure for the pupils to deal with their new surroundings of learning in such a way, and more than that, the project encouraged a deeper emotional anchorage of the school ship. And whenever the kids see us together – 'us' meaning the two of us who have organised the project – they ask, 'When will we do something like that again?'

Children's voices

It is time now to deal with another aspect of evaluation: what makes us (teachers or researchers) believe that our pupils feel the same about evaluation projects as we do? There are a few ways to discover their real feelings – for example, by asking them to write down their impressions. Here are a few of their brief comments:

My thoughts on Steffi and her team: it looks untidy, and there are too many kids in the pictures, you cannot see the places they have chosen.

It comes out very well on the poster, what I always feel when I am in this place!

The kitchen itself doesn't stink, only sometimes the food makes you sick.

Why did their hair stand on end *outside* the physics lab? Has there been an experiment?

What is so fascinating about standing on the dusty staircase that leads to the loft?

I feel happy in this school, but a number of things need to be changed!

It is clear that there are many differing opinions as to what is perceived and what pupils like or dislike. This makes it difficult to propose or to implement straightforward and agreed change. So we are led to the next question – about the process which, simply through awareness raising, was in itself a change process. For example, Angelica wrote: 'We came to know each other much better while we took the photographs, and it was very interesting for me to see where the others liked to be and where not', and Tanja added, 'You had to think over the reasons for liking or hating a room very precisely and profoundly'. And this is what Christof thought: 'You made friends with more children because you had to negotiate everything among the members of the group, and then you had to find a compromise about what to write on the poster'.

Melanie mentioned another aspect: 'I can tell precisely who enjoyed taking part in the project and who looked bored – the former try to create many different views and have funny ideas, the latter look the same all the time'. Melanie, who does not like to have her own photograph taken, did enjoy this aspect of working in the team: 'I really don't like to smile and have a picture taken of me, but I like the work in the group a lot'.

Vedrana wrote down on her feedback sheet: 'I liked the idea because I think that our school could definitely be made to look better, for example, the tables should be polished and cleaned. The procedure was OK, everybody could say frankly what his or her opinion was'. But she also felt unhappy when she noticed that some of her classmates did not listen to the viewpoints of the others: 'If you get such a chance to change things in your school, then you have to pay attention! And if you are going to change things, you might as well change the whole thing, not just half of it!'

Patricia wrote: 'Interesting topic, I hope a lot of things will be changed! The procedure did not cause any problems'. Her friend Maja added 'Almost no differences of opinion!', but another question had become pertinent for her: 'We only spoke about all the things we could have changed without spending lots of money on it'. Another member of this group wrote: 'The project is really super! If we start quarrelling over who is going to write what on the poster, we try to sort it out among ourselves anyway'.

Another group was not so successful in reaching consensus at the beginning, but they did solve their problems in the end: 'We could not agree for quite a long time, but at last we have managed it. We want to be in the same group next time'. But there were some critical voices among the pupils, too: 'The topic seemed a little bit odd and difficult to me. We had to discuss this, there were different opinions on the procedure and I could not succeed in persuading the members of my group!'

So we should keep in mind what they have learned from this evaluation project; to put it briefly, it *is* difficult (and at the same time it *is* necessary) to cope with the 'darker sides of democracy'!

What we have learnt for future photo evaluations

In order to prevent anyone interested from having to invent the wheel for a second time, the following tips might help to start the process of photo evaluation:

- Make sure that the setting will produce usable evaluation results, for instance by watching the process of decision making in the groups. Who are the opinion leaders and outsiders?
- Keep an eye on time resources – one lesson will not be long enough, of course, and all groups must be able to take their pictures without time pressure. On the other hand it makes no sense to provide too many pictures or too much time for each group. An important part of the learning process is how to deal with the limited time available within the school setting.
- Take into consideration how old the pupils are. You might think about involving two teachers to help the pupils while working in groups.
- Use only one camera and have the pupils prepare a list with a detailed plan of the procedure: who is going to take which photos? (If some of the pupils are allowed to use their own cameras you will hardly ever get all the photographs in the classroom at the same time, because they might not be developed simultaneously! It is important to have all the photos ready for the further stages in the project.)
- The project can evoke strong emotions. The message of the question 'Where do you feel happy in school and where not?' is this: it is of importance what *you* (the pupils) think and feel about things. It is worth documenting by taking photographs and by making these public – so, as a teacher, don't be worried if they get deeply involved in their 'jungle of feelings'.
- Another difficulty: decision making in the groups needs maturity as well as communication skills and tolerance of conflict. On the other hand the project offers you the opportunity to deal with communication and conflict resolution and learning by doing. The whole project may develop into a lesson on how to handle conflicts and emotions for pupils – and teachers!
- One more aspect we would like to mention here: corporate identity is stimulated by the project, especially if the pupils decide to take responsibility for the consequences of what they have found out about their situation. Teachers should be prepared for this, too.

Moving between different layers of reality

According to constructivist theory we do not regard human behaviour as following a simple cause-effect relationship (see Glasersfeld 1997: 124). Rather, we tend to see it in its entirety, its elements interwoven in a network of interrelationships, each influencing the causes of all the others. Therefore it is a study of social significance – that is, how events and rules of interactions become meaningful within the overall framework of reference, signifying the changes within the overall system and the very structures of the system (see Simon 1993: 26).

There is not only one 'reality' in an organisation like a school, but multiple realities. Taking photographs offers a challenging opportunity to bring to the fore the different layers of reality of the 'school world'. So, the camera provides a special lens which can be focused on the single elements of school life by alternating between the foreground and the background and thus enabling apparently 'unimportant details' to become the main focus of interest.

Aspects of the micro system of a school can be disarranged by isolating elements from the whole, so that they can be viewed from a different angle. Thus, in the picture taken by the pupils, the head's office is no longer the administrative centre of the school, but commented on as 'not a friendly place because behind that door there are dangers lurking'. For the children the staff room is not, as it is for the teachers, the only retreat to their professional community, but 'the place where boring lessons come from'. As in everyday life, there is no 'real' reality (see Watzlawick *et al.* 1969) and no comprehensive human consensus, but only islands of agreement in a sea of different opinions (see Simon 1993: 61).

So, what are the relevant layers of reality which we came to know through the photographic lenses in the project described?

The 'soft' reality of the worlds of pupils and teachers

In the first place, taking pictures builds a bridge to the pupils's everyday lives, especially as regards young people's feelings, because usually they perceive a deep abyss between their own priorities and those of adults. Consequently, they experience an intense discrepancy between the appreciation of parts of life through their own experience and through 'official' attitudes. On the one hand they are preoccupied with their own central themes such as:

- Can I keep up with the others in collecting and swapping stickers and do I have the posters of the 'right' pop groups?
- Will I be asked to join when schoolmates meet in the afternoon? And, am I an active player in the game of who goes out with whom? Or will I be left out?
- Will I be accepted by X in discussions during the break or am I accepted as a competent volleyball player and therefore quickly

a part of the clique that huddles together at break times? Or will I be chosen for the team? Or do I have to feel like a minor player?

• Can I afford to have a different opinion from what the 'significant others' in class think about a certain sport or question of fashion, or even have a different view of a certain teacher? Or should I howl with the pack?

On the other hand, they experience on a continuing basis how that very world is deprecated in the official school curriculum. They are acutely aware of how it is forgotten or, at best, tolerated, on the understanding that it does not interfere with the world of adult values! In the official school curriculum, questions look different from those which children and young people ask in their everyday world of schooling. They usually follow the pattern I-R-E – teacher initiates, pupil responds, teacher evaluates 'correct' or 'incorrect' (Schratz and Mehan 1993). They are typical school questions, to which the correct answer is already known and which form the basis for the universal pattern of teaching. They serve the purpose of conveying functional knowledge for surviving the (future?) challenges of life. According to Horst Rumpf (1987) teaching of that kind leads to a 'desolation of the learning culture'.

However, when pupils move through the school building taking photographs, by discussing and reflecting 'in the jungle of feelings' this fine distinction between learning questions and life questions is partially remediated. In trying to find the unknown in the known and to sense where relationships exist between their school world and their world of feelings, *their own* views begin to count. What is important is how *they* feel. In the course of the project they are asked to articulate those feelings and make them accessible, a further element in the process even if it doesn't necessarily lead to change.

By undertaking this kind of action research through taking photos, pupils (and teachers) have the opportunity to interrupt the teaching routine according to the I-R-E pattern described above. Pupils start asking questions to which the teachers do not have answers. There is no evaluation referring to 'correct' or 'incorrect', no prescribed curriculum, and pupils' opinions have to be taken seriously. This can mean a first step towards a relationship of trust, which is a necessary prerequisite for lasting experiences. According to Senge (1990), this enduring state only comes into existence when there is trust, acceptance and synergy all contributing to a common goal. This also means a first step towards a 'learning school', a school which organises its own process of development through a social architecture which involves teachers, pupils, heads, parents, non-teaching staff and others (see Ekholm *et al.* 1995: 80).

The 'hard' reality of the physical surroundings

On another level the medium of photography renders itself to (self) reflection on the *actual infrastructure* and the *shortcomings* of the *school building*. This is demonstrated, for example, by the unanimously acclaimed acceptance of the plain little school yard, which the pupils are allowed to use once a day for a quarter of an hour, assuming it is a good day during the warm season.

According to Foucault (1976), schools are organisations which are founded on the principle of 'closed institutions' and are built around control and punishment as sanctioning mechanisms. Schools are included among institutions which are seen as organisations of mistrust, in which a permanent surveillance of the pupils takes place. To them, taking photographs means a temporary liberation from this control of teacher surveillance, which they may use according to their own imaginations within the school premises. It is not surprising that several photos depict ways out of this surveillance situation.

Freezing objects in the pictures, however, should not only be an occasion for beginning to reflect on and exchange experiences of different feelings. More than that, the results of the project, in particular the comments which the pupils wrote about their photos, were intended to start participants thinking about how some of the changes in the organisation of a school day, or what changes in the infrastructure of the building, might be possible (e.g. a second break in the day to be spent outside).

The photo documents are harder 'facts' than individual expressions by pupils, which often do not even reach the ears of the person in charge. In this form they become important pieces of testimony for living out forgotten (or suppressed?) reasoning. Hence the project also served emancipatory claims. How can we contribute to making our own issues work in the way we want to see them work? This is no longer a learning question but a question of survival – in a time when the identity of the individual has become more and more absorbed by the process of civilisation (Elias 1996). Although the steps taken by the pupils are only timid, as trace elements they can gain momentum through the photos taken, beginning to set in train further steps.

Pupils conducting research into their workplace confront their teachers with the 'hard realities' of the context of their learning experiences. These are not minor aspects of school life, as we have heard them called by some people. A mere attitude of 'You can't change things anyway!' expresses an externally visible resignation which is often mirrored in a negative attitude. If we do not take seriously pupils' requests in the area of the 'hard' architecture we will also fail in those attempts which are related to the social architecture of the school. The more pupils identify with their school, the more they also assume responsibility for it. An impressive example is a 'school for truants' in Britain. Pupils who had been regular truants in their previous school had a strong allegiance to the school they had built up together with a caring teacher.

Although it is often difficult to influence changes in the building site itself within the state school system, there are different ways of reacting to pupils' wishes. In our experience these range from the local educational authorities not allowing ugly concrete walls to be painted on to providing the pupils with a common room of their own which they could declare off limits to teachers – mirroring the sign 'No entry for pupils' on the door leading into the staff room. In most schools there is a wide enough latitude for decision making *between* those positions to let the pupils feel that they also have a say in the school's autonomous development. This, of course, should also be true for the teachers, who also need to experience a feeling of 'owning' their school.

Realities in the making

Our society is highly dominated by the culture of the word. Therefore writing takes a high (if not the highest) priority in the school curriculum, which is also shown in the dominance of the subject area (see e.g. the role of language and orthography). With the increasing relevance of education the non-verbal culture has lost influence in learning, because in 'teaching in general and in the final exams of schools and universities, which are decisive for the social future, both the verbal culture and the intelligence manifested in the written word persistently dominate' (Rumpf 1987: 32, our translation).

Therefore the knowledge to be acquired is not open to challenge but instead remains an instrument of dominance which has to be assimilated (and further reproduced) within the framework of socialisation and selection. Mr Keating, the teacher in the cult movie *Dead Poets' Society*, tried to break out of this socialisation process by tearing pages out of classic books prescribed for his pupils. Mere *deconstruction* itself, however, does not in itself lead to an enhancing educational process. It is necessary to *reconstruct* cultural knowledge in such a way that it becomes accessible and can be challenged and manipulated. For this purpose photography is a medium which grasps reality in its *whole complexity* as a frozen image.

According to Susan Sontag (1979: 88) photos are not only evidence of what an individual sees, not just documents but an evaluation of the world (view). Therefore they present a 'vision' of the relationship between subjects and objects, which manifests itself in the snapshot. The interconnectedness between places, rooms, areas and feelings, emotions and associations has received little attention in pedagogics, and even less in schooling where teaching is mainly based on cognitive aspects of the curriculum (see Hierdeis and Schratz 1992).

Compared with filming and video, photography as a medium lives from the conscious separation of particular elements (such as language or movement) and asks for the intensification of the remaining possibilities, such as focusing on the sense perception of the Gestalt, the appreciation of the strangeness in the familiar culture, through the perspective framed by the camera lens. What is distant in thoughts suddenly comes close and becomes accessible through the process of focusing.

Horst Rumpf (1986: 135) put this question: where else can we learn how to live with the irritation caused by seeing reality differently and noticing that things do not always look the way one wants them to, if not through school and university? Yet, according to him, both institutions seem to do everything they can to exclude such irritants, because only then can you achieve membership in the community of specialists.

Apart from the practical value to the pupils and teachers involved, using photographs has an added value for theory building. On the one hand, the experience brings new insights into research of teaching and learning, as different aspects run together in an interdisciplinary way through photography (e.g. the connection of the areas of media education, educational sociology, teaching German and the arts, evaluation as part of educational studies). In this sense photographs cannot just be appropriated by a single subject area, because they grasp the experience of schooling in its whole complexity by means of a snapshot.

The same is true for the value of photography as a research instrument in academia. In the domain of the social sciences the visual aspect has been largely excluded from the research discourse, although it is entirely relevant to the social sciences. Through their strong empirical orientation they have sought to fulfil the scientific criteria of objectivity, reliability and validity rather than developing their own methodologies for dealing with the social aspects of everyday life.

Social scientists tend to view photos sceptically because they carry manifold meanings and can therefore be manipulated easily. But it is for this very reason that we think such visual media are well suited to enhancing understanding of the complexity of social relationships. For example, we think that the pupils' photos explain a lot about the human aspects of school life, which are less accessible through other research methods, as they contribute to making visible the invisible (see Schratz and Walker 1995).

Making the invisible visible has a compelling character; photos start people talking and require them to reflect on the 'reality' of the people or situations which they depict, because all photographic events are manifold except for those whose personal relation to the event creates the continuity which 'is not there' (see Berger and Mohr 1982: 128). Therefore, on one level, they contribute to bringing the pupils into discussion with each other about their personal relationship to the situations depicted in the pictures. At another level the teacher is confronted with *their* motifs and *their* emotional responses, so gaining access to pupils' experience of their school reality.

The reflections initiated by such a project, which usually do not occur often enough during the routines of everyday schooling, can initiate a chain reaction: other classes are motivated to find and present the places where *they* feel (un)happy. Teachers suddenly realise that they have not given sufficient thought to how they themselves feel about their workplace. In this sense the photos produced by the pupils are a valuable instrument of internal self-evaluation. This is not something done by an external researcher, but by pupils, encouraged to conduct research into their own situation with the aim of improving the condition of their own social life in school (see Elliott 1991).

In this sense, taking photos is a valuable medium in action research, especially when used in this way by pupils. The reactions of teachers from all types of school and from universities to our first reports and presentations have reassured us that we have broken new ground, although a ground already prepared for us by other colleagues. We have received many new suggestions, for which we wish to express our wholehearted thanks. This goes first and foremost to the pupils involved who have opened up for us new insights about school, teaching and learning and their development.

At the beginning of this chapter we argued for photo evaluation as a means of gaining access to the inner world of schools from the pupils' perspective. This, of course, opens up the question of ownership: is it really the pupils who want this evaluation to happen? How much of 'self' is left in their efforts to evaluate the culture of their school? Is it not us, the facilitators (teacher and researcher) who have a vested interest in photo evaluation taking place? And with what aim? We are aware that we cannot simply break through this existing power relationship by simply providing pupils with a camera. Their photos do not tell the 'full story'. They are part of a larger story which points at the dilemma which continually confronts post-structuralist research: institutional settings, and schools in particular, are not arenas in which individuals are able to freely decide on their own actions. Although pupils have been able to break through the institutional conventions by using the medium of photo evaluation, they are still pupils who have to follow their teacher's instructions. Nonetheless, if teachers provide them with the instruments which help them to be better at expressing themselves, it does serve to lend them a more robust political voice.

We do not think that schools or other 'closed' institutions are trust organisations to start with. Historically, schools have been institutions of learning based on the written word in order to safeguard orthodoxy in the reproduction of society. Therefore a 'one off' project in photo evaluation can have a minimal effect on a school's culture, despite the power of this approach. In a systems change sense, it is important to build photo evaluation into the culture of an organisation so that it becomes part of an ongoing aspect of the school calendar.

In a European project on self-evaluation (MacBeath *et al.* 2000) many of the 101 schools involved tried out photo evaluation. At the end of the project a workshop was conducted to find out how schools had put photo evaluation into practice in their respective countries. Presentations from different countries demonstrated a variety of different approaches to the use of this technique. The workshop also served the purpose of reaching a new understanding of the methodology and suggesting innovative ways of approaching it in the future. Thus new ideas were presented for the use of photo evaluation such as:

- indicators of pupil well-being;
- the quality of communication between pupils, between pupils and teachers and between school and community;
- indicators on the state of school democracy;
- teaching styles which support or inhibit pupils' learning processes;
- the acceptance of a 'new culture of curiosity and learning' among the teaching staff;
- the condition of the school buildings;
- the surroundings of the school.

The methodology of photo evaluation does not sit neatly within an effectiveness paradigm. It defies easy quantification or reduction. Our experience convinces us, though, that it can be a powerful strategy for school improvement.

References

Berger, J. and Mohr, J. (1982) *Another Way of Telling*. London: Writers and Readers.
Ekholm, M., Meyer, H., Meyer-Dohm, P., Schratz, M. and Strittmatter, A. (1995) *Wirksamkeit und Zukunft der Lehrerfortbildung in Nordrhein-Westfalen. Abschlußbericht der Evaluationskommission.* Düsseldorf: Kultusministerium.
Elias, N. (1996) *Über den Prozeß der Zivilisation*, vol. 1. Frankfurt: Suhrkamp.
Elliott, J. (1991) *Action Research for Educational Change*. Milton Keynes, UK: Open University Press.
Foucault, M. (1976) *Überwachen und Strafen. Die Geburt des Gefängnisses.* Frankfurt: Suhrkamp.
Glasersfeld, E.v. (1997) *Wege des Wissens. Erkundungen durch unser Denken.* Heidelberg: Carl Auer.
Hierdeis, H. and Schratz, M. (eds) (1992) *Mit den Sinnen begreifen. 10 Anregungen zu einer erfahrungsorientierten Pädagogik.* Innsbruck: Österreichischer StudienVerlag.
MacBeath, J., Schratz, M., Meuret, D. and Jakobsen, L. (2000) *Self-Evaluation in European Schools – A Story of Change*. London: Routledge/Falmer.
Meyer, H., Meyer-Dohm, P., Schratz, M. and Strittmatter, A. (1995) *Wirksamkeit und Zukunft der Lehrerfortbildung in Nordrhein-Westfalen. Abschlußbericht der Evaluationskommission.* Düsseldorf: Kultusministerium.
Prosser, J. (1998) *Image-based Research: A Sourcebook for Qualitative Researchers*. London: Falmer Press.
Rumpf, H. (1986) *Mit fremdem Blick. Stücke gegen die Verbiederung der Welt.* Weinheim: Beltz.
Rumpf, H. (1987) *Belebungsversuche. Ausgrabungen gegen die Verödung der Lernkultur*, München: Juventa.
Schratz, M. and Mehan, H. (1993) Gulliver travels into a math class: in search of alternative discourse in teaching and learning, *International Journal of Educational Research*, 19: 247–64.
Schratz, M. and Walker, R. (1995) *Research as Social Change: New Possibilities for Qualitative Research*. London: Routledge.
Senge, P.M. (1990) *The Fifth Discipline: The Art & Practice of the Learning Organization*. New York: Currency Doubleday.
Simon, F.B. (1993) *Meine Psychose, mein Fahrrad und ich. Zur Selbstorganisation von Verrücktheit.* Heidelberg: Carl Auer.
Sontag, S. (1979) *On Photography*. Harmondsworth, UK: Penguin.

Walker, R. (1993) Finding a silent voice for the researcher: using photographs in evaluation and research, in M. Schratz (ed.) *Qualitative Voices in Educational Research*, pp. 72–92. London: Falmer Press.

Watzlawick, P., Beavin, J.H. and Jackson, D.D. (1969) *Menschliche Kommunikation. Formen, Störungen, Paradoxien*. Bern: Huber.

7 Democratic leadership in an age of managerial accountability

Jorunn Møller

Introduction

Democratic leadership is a concept charged with positive feelings and connotations. Most people in Scandinavia would probably agree to the need for democratic leadership in schools, but clearly there will be disagreement about how democratic leadership is defined and how it should be provided. For instance, based on an analysis of the history of Swedish education, Tomas Englund (1986) has given evidence of the ongoing struggle between different conceptions of democracy. The educational concept which is dominant at any given time can be said to constitute the outer framework defining what is educationally possible in ideological terms. Even in the wider society the meaning of democracy is ambiguous, and that makes it even more difficult to agree to its meaning for everyday life in schools. The key question is what a worthwhile and valuable education, based on democratic principles, should look like, and what the consequences are for leadership in schools.

The vision of a democratic school

There has been extensive theorising in social theory about issues of democracy and the relationship between society and education. John Dewey's (1937) writings about the 'lived democracy' and his vision of a Great Community have had a significant influence. The discussions of deliberative democracy owe a great deal to the work of Jürgen Habermas' (1987) theory of communicative rationality and Hanna Arendt's (1958) theorising about a provisional community where the public space is fundamentally identified with plurality. Michael Apple (2000a) has elaborated the analysis of the relationship between society and education with the conception of a critical democracy, focusing on who is included within a community and who is left out. He underscores that a community is always constituted in specific historical conditions and against a background of political interests.

Key points of reference in this chapter are John Dewey's (1937) writings about the 'lived democracy' and Michael Apple's (2000) analysis of the conditions on which a democratic school depends.

For the notion of democratic leadership, Dewey's writings serve as an important vision and inspiration. In 'Democracy and educational administration' (1937: 345–6) he wrote:

> What the argument for democracy implies is that the best way to produce initiative and constructive power is to exercise it. Power, as well as interest, comes by use and practice . . . The delicate and difficult task of developing character and good judgement in the young needs every stimulus and inspiration possible . . . I think, that unless democratic habits and thought and action are part of the fibre of a people, political democracy is insecure. It cannot stand in isolation. It must be buttressed by the presence of democratic methods in all social relationships.

In other words, if students attending school are to develop a democratic way of life, there are certain conditions that must be in place so that they are offered the opportunities to learn what that way of life means and how it might be led. First, the curriculum must emphasise giving young people democratic experiences. Second, it is important to establish democratic structures and create processes by which life in the school is carried out. The best way to teach and learn democracy, Dewey says, is to practise it. This presupposes that the same kind of democratic habits, thoughts and actions we want students to develop have to characterise the relationships between teachers and school principals.

In *Democratic Schools: Lessons from the Chalk Face*, Michael Apple and James Beane (1999: 7) discuss the conditions on which a democracy depends. In order to develop democratic schools the following conditions must be present:

- the open flow of ideas, regardless of their popularity, that enables people to be as fully informed as possible;
- faith in the individual and collective capacity of people to create possibilities for resolving problems;
- the use of critical reflection and analysis to evaluate ideas, problems and policies;

- concern for the welfare of others and 'the common good';
- concern for the dignity and rights of individuals and minorities;
- an understanding that democracy is not so much an 'ideal' to be pursued as an 'idealised' set of values that we must live by and that must guide our life as people;
- the organisation of social institutions to promote and extend the democratic way of life.

In other words, if schools are meant to be democratic places, the idea of democracy must extend to the many roles adults play in schools. Democracy requires the creation of specific structures – democratic thoughts and attitudes must characterise the relationship between those who work in schools and the relationship between the school and the local community.

We must live this set of democratic values. But as we all know, schools have been rather undemocratic institutions throughout history, despite the rhetoric of democracy in our society (see Beane and Apple 1999).

The governing of the Norwegian school

National objectives for the Norwegian education service stress the importance of providing equal access to education regardless of domicile, sex, social or cultural background and abilities. There is no streaming according to abilities, gender or other factors. When examining the Norwegian core curriculum, one will find most of the conditions mentioned by Apple and Beane (1999) present in the text. For instance it says:

Education should be based on the view that all persons are created equal and that human dignity is inviolable. It should confirm the belief that everyone is unique; education should foster equality between sexes and solidarity among groups and across borders (p. 7).

Education should view individuals as moral beings, accountable for their decisions and responsible for their actions; with the ability to seek what is true and to do what is right. But individuals are also capable of behaving destructively, in defiance of their conscience, contrary to norms, against better judgement, and to the detriment of themselves and others. Education must therefore authenticate society's ideals and values and enliven them so that they become a potent force in people's lives (p. 9).

Critical judgement in different areas of life should be developed by testing expression and performance against specific standards (p. 14).

Further, it is underscored that teachers should function as role models for children, as a community of colleagues who share responsibility for the pupils' development, and work with parents, other professionals and the authorities. The consequences for leadership in school are highlighted in the text in a more general way, and emphasis is given to how the school principal as an employer must enhance and assure teachers' opportunities to flourish and thrive:

> the co-ordination of effort and collaboration among colleagues is decisive for the results that are achieved. This places new demands on the school's leadership. Teachers' opportunities to thrive and flourish presuppose vigour and verve, as well as an employer who appreciates the intrinsic and vital requirements of the teaching profession (p. 24).

In other policy documents it is emphasised that democracy and democratic attitudes should be one of the keystones of primary, secondary and adult education (Parliament Proposal No. 15, 1995/6).

Even though devolution of decision making to schools has been widely advocated, schools have worked to fairly detailed curriculum guidelines in terms of timetable and syllabuses. At the same time there has been a strong norm of non-interference in the teacher's classroom activities, and individual autonomy is part of the tradition in schools and related to the history of teaching in Norway. Trust in teachers' work has long been a tacit dimension in principals' approach to leadership, establishing accepted zones of influence (Berg 1996). However, established zones of control are now challenged, as some parents and people outside schools question the individual autonomy each teacher has in their classroom.

Discourses of democratic leadership

Within much of the international research in the field of educational administration, 'effective' school leaders are generally characterised as strong, decisive, directive, proactive and visionary. At the same time they are, by comparison with principals in general, also described as open and collaborative. But will 'effective' school leaders, within this way of framing it, also serve a democratic vision in line with a Deweyan perspective? That should imply advocating a 'power with' leadership orientation. However, principals identified as 'effective' are generally described in terms of a 'power over' or 'power through' rather than a 'power with' leadership orientation.

Only to a small degree do these studies provide evidence that teachers, students and parents receive opportunities to participate fully in democratic decision making at the school level (see Blase *et al.* 1995). For instance, transformational leadership as described by Leithwood *et al.* (1996) can be interpreted as a form of strong, charismatic and visionary leadership that emphasises cultural rather than bureaucratic control over teachers. Control through more subtle cultural and ideological means might be an effective leadership strategy, but is it democratic? The individual who has formal power is willing to share powers, but only at their discretion.

Critical theorists, such as Gary Anderson (1996), Michael Apple (2000a), Richard Bates (1990), Joseph Blase (Blase *et al.* 1995) and William Foster (1986), have attempted to develop a democratic theory of power that leads to a 'power with' model of leadership in which leading and following is a fluid, interactive and reciprocal process. They have contributed to analyses of educational politics with accounts of the daily subtle negotiations that occur behind the scenes. These accounts show how teachers, students, parents and school leaders struggle with each other over the meaning of the school. Educational institutions provide contexts in which identities are continuously constructed and reconstructed. In order to capture adequately the complicated and dynamic nature of school life, they advocate that an alternative approach to research is needed. This is a *micro-political* perspective. This approach will not produce a universal list of what characterises a democratic leader, but hopefully it will enhance a better understanding of what goes on in schools and give examples of the conditions on which a democracy depends and in which it might be established in different contexts.

Examples are given in the book *Democratic Principals in Action* (Blase *et al.* 1995), where the authors have presented a series of portraits of eight principals struggling to move towards more democratic forms of school administration. When the book was published all the school principals were members of the League of Professional Schools in Georgia. This league's purpose was to establish democratic decision-making structures to promote teacher involvement in school-wide instructional and curricular decisions. The eight principals' stories did not represent perfect role models. On the contrary, these principals were not perfect, and shortcomings and confusions were apparent among them all. Their stories do however show that democratic leadership can be framed differently, depending on the people involved and the context, and that they were struggling daily to fulfil their vision. However, they did have the following orientations in common:

- they all tried to encourage teachers' involvement in decision making about instruction and are committed to the principle of sharing power with others;
- they were all child-centred and strongly committed to improving teaching and learning, and to supporting teachers;
- they all had trust in teachers' motives;
- they all had the ability to listen and to communicate openly.

Their personal satisfaction was linked to seeing growth in teachers and programmes. They talked about the pride they felt because of what they had achieved from working together. But relationships with school boards were problematic. Principals were caught between traditional central office expectations and teachers' new expectations for participation in decision making. Transforming organisational and cultural structures required a great deal of time over the long term. There was no quick fix.

School principals are leaders of highly educated people carrying out intellectual and emotional work. To be able to lead such a group in a democratic way, the leader him or herself must be a learner (Moos *et al.* 2000). That requires official arenas for collaboration between teachers, school principals, parents and other stakeholders, where decisions affecting the school and the education of students can be discussed and treated as a continuous learning process. Stories, like the ones from the League of Professional Schools in Georgia, might be used as mirrors for reflections about the meaning of being a professional and of being accountable to the different constituencies, both among people working in the school, and between the school and other educational stakeholders.

A professional teacher or professional school principal is accountable to society and to many different constituencies. As professionals they try to find ways of explaining achievements and failings in recognition of the need to build trust in practice and in judgements made about practice. As Sockett (1993: 17) has framed it, 'professions work within some moral vision of human betterment, some set of professional ideals which describe the moral purpose of the enterprise'.

The dominance of managerial accountability

Both politicians and top administrators in Norway, as well as in many other countries, have recently argued that teachers are making claims on behalf of their clients, or perhaps rather on behalf of their own interests as a group. Politicians use the notion of 'provider capture' implying that those who provide the service capture the benefit (Lawton 1992). This may be the reason why external evaluation of education at various levels has come to the fore in recent years. According to many politicians and chief executives, education policy can no longer be based on widespread trust in the professional competence of educators, and teachers' performance should be controlled and judged according to criteria established outside the profession.

The discourses surrounding schools are changing. Managerial accountability is becoming more dominant, and that means that the context for democratic forms of leadership is changing. The OECD (Organisation for Economic Cooperation and Development) has played a powerful role in transforming the model of accountability, which is now becoming more and more dominant. Through the IEA (International Association of the Evaluation of Educational Achievement) they have implemented large-scale international comparisons such as TIMSS (Third International Math and Science Study) and PISA (Programme for International Student Assessment). These comparative studies try to combine contradictory elements, on the one hand establishing universal standards of quality and comparing achievements in accordance with these standards in different countries, and on the other hand encouraging participating countries to learn from each other and open up their practice to critical reflection in relation to their own priorities.

All too easily these international league tables seem to be used by politicians to put additional pressure on the school system in all countries. Teachers and school principals are subject to pressure from governments to improve national ranking in the different subjects. Improving the ranking becomes an aim in itself, not the efforts to understand and discuss how schooling could be improved, and what goals are most important to achieve. Thus, these studies have a global effect and influence the way all countries define quality, including developing and poor countries, which do not participate in the international rankings. The problem is that the information gained from these studies is often 'too technically flawed to serve as an accurate measure of national effectiveness' (Brown 1998: 33).

Jill Blackmore (2001) argues, and I agree, that this new educational accountability has been more about regulation and performance than educational improvement, local capacity building and the encouragement of democracy in schools. Thus, the bureaucratic state has been changed into the evaluative state. There has also been a shift in the language which we use. We have moved away from broader notions of social justice including issues of ethnicity, race, class and disability to more individualised notions of merit, diversity and choice. Debates about equity have been reframed within debates about literacy, which are in turn driven by an outcome-based approach based on standardised testing. According to Blackmore, the focus upon performance indicators has served managerial purposes because it is more about international ranking than about explaining school differences. Longitudinal studies demonstrate that no organisation is effective in all areas, for all students all the time.

In a similar vein, Judyth Sachs (2001) has argued that there seem to be at least two competing discourses influencing the professional identity of teachers and school principals. These discourses, which she calls *managerial* and *democratic professionalism*, set limits on what can be said, thought and done with respect to debates and initiatives about professionalism in schools. The managerial discourses, Sachs notes, claim that efficient management can solve any problem and that practices that are appropriate for the private sector can be applied to the public sector as well. This gives rise to a competitive ethos rather than a collaborative one. Democratic professionalism goes far beyond individual autonomy for teachers and has at its core an emphasis on collaborative actions between teachers, school principals, students and other educational stakeholders. It seeks to demystify professional work and build alliances between teachers, students and the members of the community in order to fulfil a democratic vision such as the one Dewey promoted. With reference to Australian experiences, Sachs argues that democratic professionalism is emerging from the profession itself, while managerial professionalism is being reinforced by employing authorities through policies on teacher professional development with their emphasis on accountability and effectiveness.

Apple (2000b) argues that we have entered a period where educational institutions are criticised, blamed and often seen as failures. He contends that in order to understand the current educational policy of conservative restoration in western countries, one has to place it in its global context. Behind the stress on higher standards, more rigorous testing and education for employment, is the fear of losing in international competition and the loss of jobs and money to Asian countries and elsewhere. The neo-liberals are currently dominant in arguing for reforms to education, and they are guided by a vision of a weak state: 'Efficiency and an "ethic" of cost-benefit analysis are the dominant norms. All people are to act in ways that maximize their own personal benefits' (Apple 2000b: 59). For the neo-liberals, 'consumer choice' is the guarantor of democracy and education will to a large degree become self-regulating if turned over to the market. In this way democracy as a political concept is transformed into an economic concept. (This also has consequences for the way we frame what we call 'democratic leadership'.) The claim is that vouchers and choice will give everyone, regardless of social class, gender and ethnicity, the right to choose among the schools that are best serving their interests. However, evidence from the USA, UK and Australia shows that the long-term effects may be to increase 'white flight' from public schools to private schools, as well as between schools and districts. The next step may be a refusal to pay taxes to support public education (Apple 2000b: 61). In a market-driven system, equity is confused with individual parent choice.

This is demonstrated in a study by Gerald Grace (1995). Building on data from a fieldwork inquiry undertaken with the cooperation of 88 school leaders in England between 1990 and 1994, he argues that there is no policy option once some principals decide to operate on market principles: 'Once a group of school leaders begins to operate upon market principles in their locality, it becomes difficult for other adjacent schools to opt-out of competitive marketing relationships' (p. 209). The moral primacy of accountability ought to be to the community, not to the market, argues Grace, and insists that 'the responsibilities of educational leadership are to build educational institutions around central values'. An important question to ask is: 'Are those central values to be those of market culture or of democratic culture?' (p. 212).

Talk about the democracy of consumers has also entered the national discourse of education and the discourse of democratic leadership in Norway. Independent of the vision of collaboration and 'lived democracy' advocated in the curriculum, the discourse of 'new public management' (NPM) seems to have a rather strong influence on how municipalities organise and govern schools in Norway, and how they talk about the governance of schools. There seems to be a change in society's values, and steps are being taken to introduce market forces into the public sector. Managerial models of administrative reform stake their claim within a definition of accountability, while language becomes an agent of ideology in shaping understanding. These changes influence the way administrators at municipal level comprehend and establish issues of accountability. The participatory discourse is over-shadowed by the administrative discourse, and so becomes distorted into a technology of control. As traditional norms of democratic accountability are progressively being questioned, the discourse of democratic leadership undergoes a gradual process of change. The values embodied in the new understanding of accountability are cost-effectiveness and efficiency.

The external quest for accountability within the Norwegian context is still limited, but lately several municipalities have outlined programmes for external evaluation of their schools. For instance, in Oslo an external evaluation system based on the Scottish system of quality assurance became effective from 1 January 2002. Delegations from many Norwegian municipalities have travelled to England, Scotland and New Zealand to learn about governance and external evaluation of schools. Different municipalities have chosen different approaches to school-based management; several of them are in fact strengthening the level of external bureaucratic control.

In accordance with trends in NPM, goals set in national curriculum guidelines are increasingly oriented toward preparing students for the workplace. School leaders could easily find themselves blindsided unless they are able to 'read' the society they serve (Moos *et al.* 2000). According to Gary Fenstermacher (1995), in many countries economic concerns are privileged over knowledge for maintaining democracy. His concern is the absence of democratic and educational ideals in contemporary educational reforms. He argues that the ideals of democracy should be included in the professionalisation process of headship, and states: 'Education and democracy are so intertwined, so critical to one another's vitality. Any loss of democratic ideals in the rhetoric and practice of educational reform is a loss of educational ideals as well' (p. 70). Therefore, principals, teachers, students and parents need to engage in critical analysis and action in order to secure democracy and contribute to economic justice. At the school site the principal will often act as the gatekeeper or the gate-opener to such analyses. However, at the same time the school principal is dependent on their relationships with the school board and other superiors, which in fact may curtail the support of democracy in schools by restricting the open flow of ideas and critical reflection. Democracy is to be supported and promoted: then the responsibility falls to people at all levels within the school system.

Conclusion

There seems to be a power struggle in society about who should define quality in schools. Both parents and students wish to make their voices heard, and other stakeholders also seek a voice in defining educational quality. As yet, however, they have had little bearing on school practice. External evaluation might address some of these issues but new problems will undoubtedly appear if the main aim turns out to be the control of teachers. In the long term, there is a risk of losing teachers' enthusiasm and commitment – a far greater problem for schools. It remains to be proved that external regulation and evaluation produce better and more democratic schools. Education cannot be developed mechanically with administrative decrees and regulations. It requires an ongoing subjective communication and negotiation.

However, continuing to fight for one's individual rights and to set one's own standards does not seem to increase public trust in the teaching profession. There is a tension between the teachers' demand for autonomy, for an independent right to draw up and discuss the ethics of professional practice, and the control of this practice by the democratic state. In order to restore and increase trust in the teaching profession, school principals and teachers need to enter the public debate with both their critiques of educational policies and their internally defined criteria of teacher professionalism. A professional role entails professional responsibility, and this implies that teachers and school leaders must make their experience more visible and public. It is important that the interaction between the *private* arena, where the teacher enjoys individual autonomy and personal responsibility for their teaching, and the *official* arena, where decisions affecting schools are made, be treated as a continuous learning process. Broader social indicators for participation and active citizenship should be used to evaluate success. In addition, there should also be a two-way accountability in which the system is accountable to schools with respect to the resources provided to adequately support them.

In this chapter I have argued that while most people underscore the need for democratic leadership in schools, there is disagreement about how democratic leadership is defined and should be provided. Thus, democratic leadership is a contested concept, and schools are sites of cultural and political struggle. Within current reform initiatives in Scandinavia as well as in other countries, I have offered some evidence to suggest that there is a risk of redefining and reconfiguring a concept like democratic leadership in economic terms rather than as a social process. Powerful interests and ideological agencies are at work to promote the market solution for educational provision and leadership. My point, with consequences for defining and framing democratic leadership, is that education's responsibilities are primarily to the democracy of citizens, rather than to the democracy of consumers (see Grace 1995). Those of us who are educators at universities have a responsibility to reveal the conditions that create social inequalities in school, including a consideration of the ways in which external social structures are reproduced through the administration of schooling. This is particularly important in an age dominated by managerial accountability. As Gary Anderson (1996: 961) has framed it, 'each of us who works in the administrative sciences must ultimately struggle to answer a key question . . . who do we work for?'

References

Anderson, G. (1996) The cultural politics of schools: implications for leadership, in K. Leithwood, J. Chapman, D. Corson, P. Hallinger and A. Hart (eds) *International Handbook of Educational Leadership and Administration*, Book 2, pp. 947–66. Dordrecht: Kluwer.
Apple, M. (2000a) *Official Knowledge: Democratic Education in a Conservative Age*, 2nd edn. New York: Routledge.
Apple, M. (2000b) Between neoliberalism and neoconservatism: education and conservatism in a global context, in N.C. Burbules and C.A. Torres (eds) *Globalization and Education. Critical Perspectives*. New York: Routledge.
Apple, M. and Beane, J.A. (eds) (1999) *Democratic Schools: Lessons from the Chalk Face*. Buckingham, UK: Open University Press.
Arendt, H. (1958) *The Human Condition*. Chicago: Chicago University Press.
Bates, R. (1990) *Educational Administration and the Management of Knowledge*. Geelong: Deakin University Press.
Beane, J.A. and Apple, M.W. (1999) The case for democratic schools, in M.W. Apple and J.A. Beane (eds) *Democratic Schools: Lessons from the Chalk Face*. Buckingham, UK: Open University Press.
Berg, G. (1996) Steering, school leadership and the invisible contract, in J. Kalous and F.v. Wieringen (eds) *Improving Educational Management* (Educational Policy and Administration Series). Akademisch Boeken Centrum, De Lier: ABC.
Blackmore, J. (2001) The implications of school governance and the 'new educational accountability' for student learning and teacher professional identity: Australian reform as an example of an 'international' problematic. Unpublished thesis, Faculty of Education, Deakin University.
Blase, J., Blase, J., Anderson, G. and Dungan, S. (1995) *Democratic Principals in Action: Eight Pioneers*. Thousand Oaks, CA: Corwin Press Inc.

Brown, M. (1998) The tyranny of the international horse race, in R. Slee and G. Weiner, with S. Tomlinson (eds) *School Effectiveness for Whom? Challenges to the School Effectiveness and School Improvement Movements.* London: Falmer Press.

Dewey, J. (1937) *Education Today.* London: George Allen & Unwin Ltd.

Englund, T. (1986) *Curriculum as a Political Problem: Changing Educational Conceptions with Special Reference to Citizenship Education*, Uppsala Studies in Education 25, Acta Universitatis Upsaliensis. Lund: Studentlitteratur.

Fenstermacher, G.D. (1995) The absence of democratic and educational ideals from contemporary educational reform initiatives, *Educational Horizons*, 73(2): 70–81.

Foster, W. (1986) *Paradigms and Promises: New Approaches to Educational Administration.* Buffalo, NY: Prometheus Books.

Grace, G. (1995) *School Leadership: Beyond Education Management – An Essay in Policy Scholarship.* London: Falmer Press.

Habermas, J. (1987) *The Theory of Communicative Action.* Cambridge: Polity Press.

Lawton, S. (1992) Why restructure? An international survey of the roots of reform, *Journal of Educational Policy*, 7(2): 139–55.

Leithwood, K., Tomlinson, D. and Genge, M. (1996) Transformational school leadership, in K. Leithwood, J. Chapman, D. Corson, P. Hallinger and A. Hart (eds) *International Handbook of Educational Leadership and Administration*, Book 2, pp. 785–841. Dordrecht: Kluwer.

Moos, L., Møller, J. and Johansson, O. (2000) A Scandinavian perspective on the culture of educational leadership. Paper presented at AERA, New Orleans, April 2000.

Sachs, J. (2001) Teacher professional identity: competing discourses, competing outcomes, *Journal of Educational Policy*, 16(2): 149–61.

Sockett, H. (1993) *The Moral Base for Teacher Professionalism.* New York: Teachers College Press.

8 Democratic leadership for school improvement in challenging contexts

Alma Harris

Introduction

There is a great deal of contemporary interest in schools in challenging contexts. However there are relatively few research studies that have focused exclusively upon effective leadership practices in such schools. In these schools, is democratic leadership appropriate, or is an autocratic style a more pragmatic solution? Is this what effectiveness and improvement require? Is it a question, as Jorunn Møller argues in Chapter 7, of 'power over' as against 'power with'?

This chapter outlines the findings from a research study funded by the National College for School Leadership that explored effective leadership in a group of secondary schools in challenging circumstances. The chapter highlights the key characteristics and features of the leadership approaches adopted and argues that the heads in the study operated a shared or distributed model of leadership. The empirical evidence from teachers, senior managers, pupils and headteachers points towards a model of leadership that is fundamentally concerned with building positive relationships and empowering others to lead. The chapter concludes by suggesting that a fundamental reconceptualisation of leadership is required that equates leadership with the many rather than the few and recognises the fundamental relationship between teacher leadership and school improvement.

The importance of leadership has been a consistent factor in school effectiveness studies and is now widely accepted as being a key constituent in achieving school improvement (Ofsted 2000). Research findings from diverse countries and different school contexts have revealed the powerful impact of leadership in securing school development and change (e.g. Velzen *et al.* 1985; West *et al.* 2000; Hopkins 2001a). Hopkins (2001b) highlights the centrality of transformational and instructional leadership practices in achieving school improvement in schools facing challenging circumstances (SFCC).

However, the literature reveals that headteachers and principals who manage change in schools in difficult circumstances are far from uniform in their leadership styles (Hallinger and Heck 1998; Lashway 1997). Early empirical studies of the kind of leadership practised by principals in American urban schools found that they differed greatly in the kind of leadership they provided (Blank 1987). Similarly, Keedy (1993) reported that a range of leadership styles was most effective in SFCC and that no single leadership approach worked in every situation.

In the USA, successive large-scale reform programmes have been aimed at low-performing and high-poverty schools (Herman *et al.* 1999). Hence a great deal of the research evidence concerning improving schools in challenging or urban contexts is derived from the American literature (e.g. Louis and Miles 1990; Louis *et al.* 1996; Elmore 2000). Only in the last few years have researchers in the UK focused their attention upon improving 'failing' or 'ineffective' schools (Barber and Dann 1996; Maden and Hillman 1996; Hopkins *et al.* 1997; Myers and Stoll 1998; Gray 2000). The most recent work in this area by Reynolds *et al.* (2001) and Hopkins (2001b) has firstly synthesised the main research evidence concerning effective improvement interventions and secondly produced a school improvement guide based upon the most successful school improvement projects and programmes.

While there is a great deal of contemporary interest in schools in difficulty, few research studies have focused exclusively upon leadership practices and approaches. Although issues of leadership inevitably feature there still remains a lack of empirical evidence concerning leadership practices in schools in difficulty. Most recently, Maden (2001) has highlighted the need for richer descriptions of leadership practices within such schools. Consequently, this research project, commissioned by the National College for School Leadership in England, focused upon leadership in schools facing difficult circumstances. Its prime aim was to contribute to the knowledge base about leadership practice within difficult school contexts.

Research design

This research project investigated leadership within a group of schools designated by the Department for Education and Skills (DfES) in England as 'facing challenging circumstances'. Schools in which 25 per cent of pupils, or less, achieve success at external examination at 16 (i.e. five or more grades A* to C at GCSE) are placed in this category. This also includes a number of schools that achieve above 25 per cent but where over 35 per cent of their pupils receive free school meals. Currently there are approximately 8 per cent of secondary schools in England in this grouping. Many of these schools are also in the DfES categories of 'special measures' or 'serious weaknesses'[1] and are subject to regular inspection. Within the SFCC group there is a high representation of schools in low socio-economic status (SES)[2] urban areas (Ofsted 2000) schools with falling roles and schools serving inner-city communities (Gray 2000).

To explore leadership approaches in these schools a research design was constructed that incorporated multiple methods. The prime aim of this approach was to capture 'thick descriptions' of leadership practice (Denzin 1979). Initially, a review of the literature relating to SFCC was undertaken in order to generate propositions and hypotheses for testing. In-depth case study data was subsequently collected from ten such schools. This included semi-structured interviews with head-teachers, middle managers and classroom teachers. In addition, a wide range of documentary and contextual data was collected at each school. The research study consisted of three phases. Phase 1 involved the literature review and generation of research questions and proposi-tions. Phase 2 involved the data collection, within-case analysis and initial reporting. Phase 3 incorporated between-case analysis and the testing of initial findings with headteachers from a group of SFCC not involved in the study.[3]

The selection of case study schools was informed by two factors. First, care was taken to ensure that the schools represented a wide range of contexts and were geographically spread. Second, inspection reports and performance data were scrutinised to ensure that there was evidence of successful leadership and an upward school improve-ment trajectory. Using this evidential base, judgements were made about 'effective leadership'. The final sample of ten schools included:

- schools located within a range of socioeconomic and cultural situations (inner city, urban, rural and those with predominantly one ethnic group, and also mixed and multiethnic groups);
- schools that were demonstrating improvement (i.e. there was evidence of improvement in performance).

In the early stages of the research clear sets of ethical and practical guidelines were agreed with participants. Over 50 interviews were conducted and these were fully transcribed. Transcripts were returned to the interviewees for correction and validation purposes. The extent of the interview data enabled in-depth, cross-case comparisons to be undertaken. This analysis led to the emergence of a number of common themes and key findings. These are outlined in the next section.

Findings

Within a study comprising of only ten schools the possibilities for generalisation are inevitably limited. However, the volume and range of data collected in this study provided a basis for some preliminary findings about leadership in SFCC to be drawn. The study aimed to explore how far leaders in such circumstances shared similar approaches to leadership and the extent to which the particular demands of the school context shaped or influenced their leadership style. Research has shown that authoritarian forms of leadership are most prevalent in schools categorised as special measures or serious weakness, particularly in the early stages (Gray 2000). In a failing school context, immediate action is required, and hence leadership approaches are often very directive and task focused. However, in schools that are not in either of the failing categories but are steadily improving, the potential for alternative leadership styles and leadership approaches clearly exists.

The evidence collected within the study suggests that headteachers adopt leadership approaches that match the particular stage of a school's development. While the heads acknowledged that they had all adopted autocratic leadership approaches at critical times they also agreed that this leadership approach was least likely to lead to sustained school improvement. The heads in the study had deliberately chosen a form of leadership to move the school forward that empowered others to lead and distributed leadership activity throughout the school. This 'teacher leadership' in many ways covers a similar terrain to transformational leadership, both in its orientation and aspiration (Leithwood and Jantzi 2000). However, the particular emphasis given by the heads to distributing leadership and empowering others would suggest an approach to leadership that has democratic rather than transformational principles at its core.

In all ten schools the research found that various forms of teacher leadership prevailed and that this directly influenced collective problem solving and decision making. While headteachers' responses to problems varied, depending on the circumstance or situation, their value position remained consistently one of empowering pupils, staff and parents. The findings from the research study suggest that leadership in SFCC is defined by an individual value system that embraces equity, empowerment and moral purpose. The study revealed a complex but compelling picture of leadership in SFCC. It reflected a form of leadership that is democratic and centrally concerned with giving others the responsibility to lead.

Vision and values

Of central importance within schools that are improving is an alignment to a shared set of values. The heads in the study communicated their personal vision and belief systems by direction, words and deeds. Through a variety of symbolic gestures and actions they were successful at realigning both staff and pupils to their particular vision of the school. The heads in the study did 'walk the talk' through the consistency and integrity of their actions; they modelled behaviour that they considered desirable to achieve the school goals; they shared a belief and had an optimism that people have untapped potential for growth and development. The heads clearly respected others and modelled teacher leadership through empowering and encouraging others. They also trusted others and required trust from others. They recognised the need to be actively supportive, caring and encouraging as well as challenging and confrontational when necessary. A consistent and shared vision was an inherent part of their leadership approach. This helped them to communicate a sense of direction for the school. As Duigan and Bhindi (1997: 29) suggest: 'Authentic leaders breathe the life force into the workplace and keep the people feeling energised and focused. As stewards and guides they build people and their self-esteem. They derive their credibility from personal integrity and "walking" their values'.

The headteachers communicated their vision through relationships with staff and students, and they built these around core values. The vision and practices of these heads were organised around personal values such as the modelling and promotion of respect for individuals, fairness and equality, caring for the well-being and whole development of students and staff, integrity and honesty. It was evident that their leadership values and visions were primarily moral – i.e. dedicated to the welfare of staff and students, with the latter at the centre. These values underpinned their relationships with staff, students, parents and governors and guided their day-to-day actions. The heads in the study did display people-centred leadership in their day-to-day dealings with individuals. Their behaviour with others was premised upon respect and trust and their belief in developing the potential of staff and students:

> The head's main aim is to allow others to flourish and grow, whether staff or students, it doesn't matter. The aim is to develop others and to generate self-belief and self-esteem in those that currently lack it.
>
> (Teacher S9)

> People are your greatest asset and I firmly believe therefore that the staff and the students in this school are my best resource for change.
>
> (Head S4)

Their ability to invite others to share and develop their vision was frequently commented upon by staff and students alike. Alongside these qualities however, were examples of heads being firm (in relation to values, expectations and standards), and, on occasion, ruthless. In many respects, the way they interacted with others was the common denominator of their success. The human qualities they possessed enabled them to lead others effectively and to establish confidence in others that their vision was worth sharing.

The heads were quick to dispel the 'cultural deficit' notion often prevalent in many SFCC and were committed to the belief that every child can learn and succeed. They made decisions that motivated both staff and students and placed an emphasis upon student achievement and learning. The heads in the study talked about 'creating the conditions that would lead to higher student performance' and they were deeply concerned about the welfare and the educational experiences of minority children. They set high expectations for students, provided clear rules about behaviour and stressed discipline. Their approach was one of empowerment through caring and through generating a culture within the school where all students were motivated to succeed.

Distributing leadership

The heads in this study adopted highly creative approaches to tackling the complex demands of implementing multiple change. The decision to work with and through teams as well as individuals was a common response to the management of change. The heads used a number of strategies for bringing out the best in staff. In addition to formal development opportunities, these strategies included: the power of praise; involving others in decision making; and giving professional autonomy. Although the heads tended to concentrate on teaching staff in the first instance, they used similar approaches when dealing with governors, parents and, to some extent, students. All the heads invested in others in order to lead the school. From the perspectives of others the overarching message was one of the head building the community of the school in its widest sense – i.e. through developing and involving others:

> When I first came to the school, the head and SMT [senior management team] were considered to be the leaders, everyone else opted out. With the formulation of teams with clear targets I've been able to distribute leadership and to energise teachers to take responsibility for change and development.
>
> (Head S7)

> The head has given real leadership responsibilities to others. It's not a case of just delegating headship tasks.
>
> (Teacher S3)

> The middle managers now have greater responsibility and authority for leading. The days of being in charge of stock cupboards are over.
>
> (SMT S10)

Heads in the study and their constituencies consistently highlighted the importance of possessing a range of leadership strategies to address the diverse sets of issues and problems they faced. They also emphasised the contingent nature of many of the decisions they made and how different leadership strategies would be used in different contexts. The majority of schools in the study had at some stage emerged from the special measures or serious weaknesses. Therefore, staff in each school had considerable experience of Office for Standards in Education (Ofsted) and Her Majesty's Inspectorate of Schools (HMI) inspection. The heads commented upon the importance of careful planning for the inspection. All the heads acknowledged that they adopted a more autocratic leadership style during the pre-inspection phase. This included paying special attention to issues such as policy implementation and consistent standards of teaching. During the inspection the heads adopted a more supportive leadership style in order to assist staff through the process. Leaders in SFCC took this role very seriously and consciously demonstrated high levels of emotional responsibility towards their staff during the inspection period. An important contributory factor to achieving a positive outcome was considered to be how the head's leadership style matched the situation or circumstances facing the school at different times:

> It's a learning curve all the time. I think leadership styles have to match the needs of that school at that particular point in time.
>
> (Head S2)

> The head displays a range of leadership styles really, much depends on the situation or circumstance.
>
> (Teacher S4)

> I don't think there is one leadership style or approach is there? Any more than there is a single teaching style. You need breadth and diversity in both.
>
> (SMT S5)

In particular the heads in this study emphasised that while they had a broad set of values they adhered to they did not consider this to be a fixed leadership approach. They felt strongly that they could switch to a leadership style that suited the situation and could behave in ways that did not reflect their core beliefs, if necessary.

Investing in staff development

A principal concern for heads in this study was one of maintaining staff morale and motivation. In a number of the schools, staff morale had been low and individual self-esteem had been eroded by successive criticism of the school. Consequently, the heads consistently and vigorously promoted staff development whether through in-service training, visits to other schools or peer support schemes. It was noticeable, also, that such development did not only focus upon needs which were of direct benefit to the school but also those which were of direct benefit to the individual. The development needs of non-teaching staff were also included. The emphasis heads placed on the continuing development of their staff was an endorsement of their belief that teachers were their most important asset and that, particularly in difficult times, it was important to maintain their own sense of self-worth by valuing them:

Teachers in this school have had their morale eroded and chipped away by successive Ofsteds. It is important to invest in them and their capabilities, to raise morale and to foster a 'can do' culture.

(Head S6)

If you are constantly told you are failing, you believe it. You are a failed teacher.

(Teacher S7)

The emphasis placed on the continuing development of their staff reflected the recognition among heads that the teachers were their most important resource. Consequently, they were highly skilled at using a combination of pressure and support to promote the efforts of teachers, particularly when working with the most difficult students. They encouraged teachers to take risks and rewarded innovative thinking.

The heads set high standards for teaching and teacher performance. The focus and emphasis upon improving teaching and learning was common across all case study schools. Time was provided to ensure that teachers met to discuss teaching and were able to observe each other teaching. In addition, teaching performance was monitored and individual assessments made. Poor teaching was not ignored or tolerated within the schools. Where it did exist, it was challenged and strategies were agreed for improvement. Where this did not occur, the necessary steps were taken by the headteacher to deal with the problem. In the majority of cases, a combination of structured support, monitoring and an individual development programme addressed the problem of poor quality teaching. For these heads, effective leadership was about capacity building in others and investing in the social capital of the school.

Relationships

The heads in this study were good at developing and maintaining relationships. They were considered to be fair and were seen as having a genuine joy and vibrancy when talking to students. They generated a high level of commitment in others through their openness, honesty and the quality of their interpersonal relationships. The heads engaged in self-criticism and were able to admit to others when they felt they had made a mistake. They placed a particular emphasis on generating positive relationships with parents and fostering a view of the school as being part of, rather than apart from, the community:

It is important that staff and students are involved in the life of the school and relate to each other in a positive way.

(Head S1)

The head has ensured that we work more in teams and work across our subject areas. This has made us build broader relationships and work together.

(Teacher S8)

Stoll and Fink (1996) describe 'invitational leadership' as a form of leadership where leaders place a high premium upon personal values and interrelationships with others. Heads in the study did reflect many of the dimensions of invitational leadership. They placed an emphasis upon people rather than systems and invited others to lead. It was clear that while they possessed a range of leadership strategies to address the diverse sets of issues and problems they faced, at the core of their leadership practice was a belief in empowering others:

Ultimately, the job of the leader is to give others the confidence and capability to take on new responsibilities. It's really about giving power to others rather than keeping it at the top.

(Head S10)

In many respects we have more power than before. We are involved in decision making, we are able to take ideas forward and to challenge new ideas and developments. I guess we are more involved, more part of the decision-making process than before.

(Teacher S6)

The head has deliberately devolved leadership to others. I was concerned at first that this would mean we would lose control over the management of the school but it has generated much more interest from the staff in being involved in decisions. There is less apathy and less resistance to change.

(SMT S5)

While the heads emphasised the contingent nature of many of the decisions they made and how different leadership strategies would be used in different contexts, the central belief in distributing leadership to teachers remained unaltered. This form of leadership starts not from the basis of power and control but from the ability to act with others and to enable others to act. It places an emphasis on allowing and empowering those who are not in positions of responsibility or authority to lead.

Community building

A distinctive feature of schools that are improving is how far they work as *a professional learning community*. Within the schools in the study a climate of collaboration existed and there was a commitment to work together. However, this climate was the result of lengthy discussion, development and dialogue among those working within and outside the school. It was deliberately orchestrated through the provision of opportunities to build social trust. This included providing opportunities for dialogue between staff and parents.

The heads in the study emphasised the need to establish an 'interconnectedness of home, school and community'. This involved communicating and understanding the needs of the community, to establish a dialogue with parents and to connect with the formal and informal community leaders. The headteachers in the study visited homes, attended community events, communicated regularly with the public about successes and engendered trust by showing care for young people. They understood the forces within the community that impeded learning, they were aware of the negative forces of the dominant culture and they listened to parents' views and opinions regularly. The heads tried to create integral relationships with the families in the communities they served. They recognised that family, school and community relationships directly affect student outcomes, hence the need to connect with the community was of paramount importance to the success of the school:

> The first thing I recognised that needed to be done was to get the parents into the school, so we screened World Cup games on parents' evenings.
>
> (Head S10)

> This school is located on the edge of a large predominantly white, working-class estate. There is long-term unemployment, low aspirations, high levels of crime and drug abuse. The biggest problem we had was getting the community to see us as a resource rather than the enemy.
>
> (SMT S3)

Within the various schools in the study there was a strong and clear commitment to academic achievement and this was regularly communicated to parents. This academic capital was developed through a commitment to the success of all pupils and a shared belief in rewarding and praising pupils. Sergiovanni (1998) points out that within schools, professional capital is created as a fabric of reciprocal responsibilities and mutual support. The heads in this study involved others in decision making and had professional trust in them. They cultivated professional dialogue among teachers, placing a high premium upon their own professional development and the professional development of their staff. In this respect, they developed professional and intellectual capital by encouraging their schools to become enquiring communities.

Another important dimension of successful leadership in SFCC is the power of context. The heads in the study were highly responsive to the demands and challenges within and beyond their own school context. In managing people and cultural change they managed external as well as internal environments. They had skills in communicating, in supporting colleagues' development so that they felt confident in fulfilling expectations of their contribution to the achievement of strategic goals and in the management of conflict and negotiating positive outcomes. In this sense, they were 'adaptive' and through these processes were able to manage conflict in a way that achieved positive outcomes.

Commentary

These research findings highlight the intensity and complexity of the leadership role in SFCC. All the heads shared high expectations and a determination to achieve the highest possible standards. They placed a high premium upon personal values and focused upon cultural rather than structural change. As Day *et al.* (2000) note, in 'rapidly changing times, technical-rational approaches to leadership may be beguilingly attractive, yet in reality are unlikely to result in improved schooling unless accompanied by both a professional and moral dimension'. It was clear from this study that the heads in these schools did not operate from a predominantly technical-rational position. They had a high degree of emotional intelligence and were acutely aware of the need to build positive relationships with pupils, teachers and parents. They did this primarily through a process of empowerment and trust, engaging pupils, parents and teachers in decision making.

In summary the research found that:

• Effective leaders in SFCC are constantly managing tensions and problems directly related to the particular circumstances and context of the school. The main leadership task facing them is one of coping with unpredictability, conflict and dissent on a daily basis without discarding core values.

• Effective leaders in SFCC are, above all, people-centred. The leadership practice of headteachers in this study was underpinned by a set of personal and professional values that placed human needs before organisational needs.

• Effective leaders in SFCC distribute leadership to others and invest in various forms of teacher leadership.

• Effective leaders in SFCC are able to combine a moral purpose with a willingness to be collaborative and to promote collaboration among colleagues, whether through teamwork or by extending the boundaries of participation in leadership and decision making.

The most important aspect of leadership for all the heads in the study concerned establishing the kinds of relationship in which their leadership could be best expressed. Being a head in a SFCC was clearly not a desk job but rather was about displaying people-centred qualities and skills. Taking this perspective, leadership is a fluid and emergent rather than a fixed phenomenon. It implies a different power relationship within the school where the distinctions between followers and leaders tend to blur. It has implications for the division of labour within a school, particularly when the tasks facing the organisation are shared more widely. It also opens up the possibility for all teachers to become leaders at various times. It implies a redistribution of power and a realignment of authority within the school as an organisation. It suggests that leadership is a shared and collective endeavour that engages all teachers within the school (Lambert 1998). It also implies that the context in which people work and learn together is where they construct and refine meaning, leading to a shared purpose or set of goals.

Silns and Mulford (2002) conclude that student outcomes are more likely to improve where leadership sources are distributed throughout the school community and where teachers are empowered in areas of importance to them. They argue that teachers cannot create and sustain the conditions for the productive development of children if those conditions do not exist for teachers. Empowering teachers in this way and providing them with opportunities to lead is based on the simple but profound idea that if schools are to become better at providing learning for students then they must also become better at providing opportunities for teachers to innovate, develop and learn together.

To cope with the unprecedented rate of change in schools in the twenty-first century requires radically new and alternative approaches to school improvement and school leadership. If schools are to be real learning communities this cannot be achieved by operating with models of change and improvement dependent upon individual or singular leadership practices. The overarching message about leadership in SFCC is one of building the community of the school in its widest sense – i.e. through developing and involving others. What characterised each of the heads in the study was their resilience, their sheer capacity for hard work and their continuing ability, under the most challenging circumstances, to provide the best opportunities for the learning and achievement of pupils and staff. They were able to convince all those within the school and the community it served that their vision was worth sharing and pursuing. In all cases they had changed their schools for the better.

Notes

1 10.6 per cent were in special measures at the end of the summer term 2000 compared to a national average of 2–3 per cent.
2 An average of 36 per cent of pupils in SFCC schools are entitled to free school meals compared to the national average of 13.5 per cent. However, the range is from 84–6 per cent.
3 National College for School Leadership seminar, October 2001.

References

Barber, M. and Dann, R. (eds) (1996) *Raising Educational Standards in Inner Cities*. London: Cassell.

Blank, R.K. (1987) The role of principal as leader: analysis of variation in leadership of urban high schools, *Journal of Educational Research*, 81(2): 69–80.

Day, C., Harris, A., Hadfield, M., Tolley, H. and Beresford, J. (2000) *Leading Schools in Times of Change*. Buckingham, UK: Open University Press.

Denzin, N.K. (1979) *Sociological Methods: A Sourcebook*. New York: McGraw-Hill.

Duigan, P.A. and Bhindi, N. (1997) Leadership for a new century: authenticity, intentionality, spirituality and sensibility, *Educational Management and Administration*, 25(2): 117–32.

Elmore, R. (2000) *Building a New Structure for School Leadership*. Washington, DC: The Albert Shanker Institute.

Gray, J. (2000) *Causing Concern but Improving: A Review of Schools' Experience*. London: DfEE.

Hallinger, P. and Heck, R.H. (1998) Exploring the principal's contribution to school effectiveness: 1980–1995, *School Effectiveness & School Improvement*, 9(2): 157–91.

Herman, R. *et al.* (1999) *An Educator's Guide to Schoolwide Reform*. Washington, DC: American Institute for Research.

Hopkins, D. (2001a) *School Improvement for Real*. London: Falmer Press.

Hopkins, D. (2001b) *Meeting the Challenge: An Improvement Guide for Schools Facing Challenging Circumstances*, London: DfES.

Hopkins, D., Harris, A. and Jackson, D. (1997) Understanding the school's capacity for development: growth states and strategies, *School Leadership and Management*, 17(3): 401–11.

Keedy, J.L. (1993) Studying principal inner realities and their practice: building the EA knowledge base. Paper presented at the annual meeting of the American Educational Research Association, Atlanta, 12–16 April.

Lambert, L. (1998) *Building Leadership Capacity in Schools*. Alexandria, VA: Association for Supervision and Curriculum Development.

Lashway, L. (1997) *Multidimensional School Leadership*. Bloomington, IN: Phi Delta Kappa.

Leithwood, K. and Jantzi, D. (2000) Principal and teacher leader effects: a replication, *School Leadership and Management*, 20(4): 415–34.

Louis, K.H. *et al.* (1996) Teachers' professional community in restructuring schools, *American Educational Research Journal*, 33(4): 757–89.

Louis, K.S. and Miles, M.B. (1990) *Improving the Urban High School: What Works and Why*. New York: Teachers College Press.

Maden, M. (2001) *Further Lessons in Success: Success Against the Odds – Five Years On*. London: Routledge Falmer.

Maden, M. and Hillman, J. (1996) *Success Against the Odds*. London: Routledge.

Myers, K. and Stoll, L. (1997) *No Quick Fixes*. London: Paul Chapman.

Ofsted (Office for Standards in Education) (2000) *Improving City Schools*. London: Ofsted.

Reynolds, D., Hopkins, D., Potter, D. and Chapman, C. (2001) *School Improvement for Schools facing Challenging Circumstances: A Review of Research and Practice*. London: DfES.

Sergiovanni, T. (1998) Leadership as pedogogy, capital development and school effectiveness, *International Journal of Leadership in Education*, 1(1): 37–46.

Silns, H. and Mulford, B. (2002) Leadership and school results, in K. Leithwood and P. Hallinger, *Second International Handbook of Educational Leadership and Administration*. Dordrecht: Kluwer.

Stoll, L. and Fink, D. (1996) *Changing Our Schools*. Buckingham, UK: Open University Press.

Velzen, W.v., Miles, M., Elholm, M., Hameyer, U. and Robin, D. (1985) *Making School Improvement Work*. Leuven: ACCO.

West, M., Jackson, D., Harris, A. and Hopkins, D. (2000) Leadership for school improvement, in K. Riley and K. Seashore Louis (eds) *Leadership for Change*. London: Routledge Falmer.

9 Learning in a knowledge society

The democratic dimension

Kai-ming Cheng

The knowledge society

Over the past two years I have been attracted by changes in the workplace and have tried to understand how such changes would affect education. In this chapter I would like to share my observations as to the major characteristics of the workplace in a knowledge society, how these characteristics are related to learning and how I think schools will be affected.

Much has been said and written about the knowledge society. But what is meant by this term? In addressing this question, my purpose is not to seek a definition but to look at real changes in society, and in the workplace in particular. I have studied large multinationals and then small- and medium-sized enterprises (SMEs) and come to the following conclusions.

General observations

First, the coming of the knowledge society is characterised by a large sector of the service economy overtaking the manufacturing industries as the major economic sector (see Figure 9.1). Second, the expansion of the service industries is mainly due to the demand for quality services which are now offered as customised services, tailor-made for varying clients. Third, the client-centred nature of such services has also led to a one-stop window of services, where total solutions are provided through integration of diverse expertise. Fourth, the concept of client-centred services has also led to the reduction of intermediate procedures in the production and delivery processes of services.

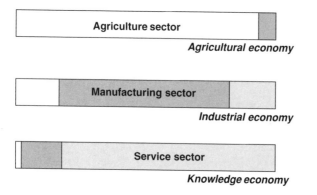

Figure 9.1 The changed economy: a symbolic shift

Newly-emerging organisations

Therefore, as old business organisations rapidly disappear in the marketplace, newly-emerging organisations fall into four broad categories:

- large firms with large numbers of clients; they include investment banks, consultancy firms and data centres, mostly diversified in their services;
- SMEs that cater for particular parts of the market with services that may vary over time;
- consortia that pool together diverse services serving the same clients;
- door-to-door supply chain services (i.e. logistics, e.g. in airport cargoes; just-in-time publishing).

The changed workplace

In this context, the organisation of the workplace has also changed (see Figure 9.2). Let us first look at the large organisations. They are few in number, but are leading the economy and hence are pioneers of changes in the workplace. In a typical large firm in the service industry, the workplace is organised in project groups, variously described as production teams, client groups, task forces or just 'accounts' (see Figure 9.3).

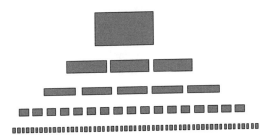

Figure 9.2 Industrial organisations: an image of hierarchy

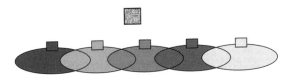

Figure 9.3 Organisation by project groups: a paradigm shift

- Such project groups are organised according to the clients in order to provide customised services to individual clients. That is, each client is served by one group, rather than by many departments.
- Each group provides a total solution to the client, such that the client does not have to deal with multiple departments of the firm.
- Such groups are largely ad hoc in nature. They change in size or nature as required and disappear when their services are no longer needed.
- Such groups replace vertical departments (where internal division of labour is the major concern) and become the major units of the organisation. Other units are subsidiary and secondary.
- Each member of the firm may work in one or more groups according to needs. They do not necessarily belong to a particular department in the traditional sense of the term.
- Members move from group to group over time, and hence constantly face non-routine expectations. They have to learn 'just-in-time', on demand.
- Groups function in teams by integration of expertise among members, with only a vague division of labour. Hence members are expected to be versatile.

- Middle management above the groups is rare and not always necessary, because most of the practical decisions about the services are made within the groups.
- There are only vague subdivisions within each group. There is usually no hierarchy within the group. Members with different experience, seniority and rank work on an equal footing.
- Boss-subordinate relations are much less intensive than interactions within groups. Hence, for example, 360 degree appraisals are conducted (i.e. from the bottom up rather than top down).
- Reward and punishment are related to eventual output rather than compliance with rules and regulations, which are few.
- Knowledge is required, and indeed is concentrated, at the front-line groups.

It has to be said that what are described above are ideal types of the contemporary workplace. Firms are structured in very different ways but most intend to move towards these ideal types. Some of them (e.g. investment banks) operate in more 'pure' forms of production groups. Others (e.g. the older consultancy firms) are in the transition from a complex 'matrix' to a neat production group structure.

If we now turn to SMEs we see that in most societies they have become the major sector of the economy. SMEs are very different in terms of size and assets when compared with large firms. However, in terms of organisation, they are quite similar. Of course they cannot afford numerous production groups, but each of them functions more or less as a production group, characterised by loose division of labour, loose hierarchy, constant change of tasks, integrated expertise, high knowledge expectation, output-oriented culture and so forth.

We can tell from the above description that the organisation of such businesses, be they large firms or SMEs in the knowledge society, is antithetical to Max Weber's ideal type of industrial organisation:

- division of labour, which is supposed to be the major merit of an industrial organisation, is no longer the accepted doctrine;
- clear lines of command, seen as essential for implementing plans from above, are now less taken for granted, not always possible and not always necessary;
- there are few layers in the organisation, and the need for middle managers is increasingly in doubt;[1]
- ranks and qualifications are much less important; knowledge is no longer attached to individuals and experience plays a much less essential role in terms of organisation.

In other words, the notion of bureaucracy, which is crucial to an industrial organisation, is collapsing.

Changed perceptions of knowledge and learning

One major characteristic of such organisations, which concerns educators, is the changed perceptions of knowledge and learning. First, unlike industrial organisations where those at the top possess the most knowledge and front-line workers are only 'operatives', it is now the front-line workers who need to possess knowledge and make decisions. Second, 'products' are designed and constructed at the front-line groups rather than manufactured according to plans handed down from the top. Third, the changing nature of the market and clients expects front-line workers to engage in just-in-time, on-demand learning of new knowledge and new skills appropriate to changing needs. Fourth, the notion of specialisation is much more blurred. There are no permanent specialists; people are expected to be versatile and work is done by integration of expertise in teams. Fifth, people are much less defined by what they have learned and what qualifications they possess – i.e. fewer and fewer people are in permanent occupations and specific 'jobs'. Sixth, success in the workplace, and for that matter personnel recruitment, looks more to the quality of people rather than the knowledge they possess. The collaborative nature of the workplace has also placed more weight on the social, moral, emotional and other non-cognitive dimensions of its members.

Assumptions in education

Such characteristics in the workplace are almost common sense and are widely assumed among working members of society, but perhaps less so among people who work in educational institutions. But the implications for education are far-reaching.

In most education systems in the world the following are largely true:

- Whether educators like it or not, the education system is expected to train manpower, and manpower is classified by specialised occupations and ranks.
- Education is a hierarchy. 'There are smart kids and dumb kids'.[2] We tend to believe that only a few can learn and hence deserve higher learning. The large majority will engage in lower-level work

– i.e. blue-collar workers who require little knowledge and little learning.

- We prepare students for occupations, such that they can become specialists in their respective fields, the more specialised the better. We offer them qualifications accordingly.
- We prepare our students by giving them knowledge. The more they possess, the better they are. How such knowledge is applied is beyond the remit of education.
- Qualifications are conceived with presumed lifelong significance. Assessment and endorsement at a certain point of life serve to label the person for the rest of their life. What is learnt later is only an extra addition.
- We prepare people to work in 'organisations' (which should read 'bureaucracies'), where each person works according to job descriptions, work plans, rule and regulations, at a specified rank.
- We continue to prepare them to work as an individual in a specific job which is realised as a position in an organisation, and to excel by fulfilling their individual task as dictated by that post. Cooperation and integration is achieved through organisational division of labour.

The above are perhaps not explicit in the minds of educators. However, our thoughts as educators often echo such assumptions by others within the realm of education. For example, that:

- knowledge exists in self-contained blocks called subjects or disciplines;
- problems are solved only within subject boundaries and not across them;
- our task is to fill students with knowledge and information;
- learning is an individual endeavour and hence individual learning outcomes are measured;
- learning takes place mainly in the classroom – anything outside the classrooms is optional and anything outside the school campus is uncontrollable and hence unfavourable;
- learning is about what teachers know and what teachers think is true or right. Learning is about what is known and what is acceptable;
- use and application of knowledge can be done only after students have been taught, and hence after 'education'.
- development of personal and interpersonal attitudes, values, or morals, is a matter for the family or the Church.

The above may seem to be unkind assertions, and perhaps not all are true in respect of any particular society. For example, there are societies where students are allowed more opportunities for exploration of new knowledge and there are other societies that pay more attention to students' personal development. However, by and large, these are assumptions that run across most sectors and most activities of education. We are so used to these assumptions that we have taken them for granted, and never feel the necessity to question them. In other words, they describe the culture of education in an industrial society.

The challenges to education

The real challenge to education, and to schools, is imminent, and the pace of change is very rapid. The above observations might not have been valid ten years ago. If we accept the above observations and further analyse what is happening in the workplace, we cannot avoid the conclusion that change is fundamental. It is not about a change in fashion that will soon be over, or something that will be sorted out by a few minor changes in policies or practice.

If the agricultural economy tied people to the land and confined people to rituals and feudal morals, then the industrial economy confines people to occupations and bureaucracies – i.e. in jobs. If the Industrial Revolution liberated human beings from the land and presumed rituals, then the knowledge society is likely to further liberate human beings from jobs, occupations and bureaucracies.

Thinking along these lines, what we have today as the education system belongs to the industrial era and will soon face a crisis because of the passing away of that era. Or, perhaps, the crisis is already there, except that we work in a protected arena so that the crisis creeps up behind us slowly and almost imperceptibly.

The general trend is a further freeing of individuals from rigid structures and preconceived career paths. In other words, there is a strong trend towards further democratisation. This means that the following predictions might have some support:

- individuals will have ready access to information and knowledge; their reliance on institutions (schools, libraries, museums etc.) for knowledge is likely to decline over time, but very quickly;
- individual learning is likely to soon transcend subject boundaries and discipline borders;
- individual learning is likely to soon transcend classrooms and campus walls;

- individuals will increasingly have more say over their own work and, therefore, over their learning;
- individuals will have increasingly more room for specific ways of constructing their own knowledge;
- fewer and fewer people will work in regular jobs and secure organisations with a stable income.

Emerging changes

Overall, institutional control of knowledge is facing a fundamental challenge. There is a general trend towards democratisation of knowledge, and hence the democratisation of the learning process. There are emerging changes that are responding to such a crisis or challenge. They all contribute positively to a new agenda for education:

- Moves in various parts of the world to expand opportunities for higher learning. Organization for Economic Cooperation and Development (OECD) countries have seen remarkable expansion at this level in the last five or six years.[3] Even in East Asia, higher education is breaking away from elitist systems.[4]
- Problem-based learning, originating in medical education,[5] which cuts across subjects and disciplines and mimics learning in the workplace.
- Moves in various parts of the world to break up the age structure of education systems.
- Moves in various parts of the world away from the partitioning of students into classes and, accordingly, unconventional designs of school buildings.
- Strong trends towards flexible learning timetables.
- Various approaches to allow students to learn beyond classrooms and campuses.
- In higher education, more variety of higher learning opportunities (e.g. online learning, non-formal learning).
- Emerging systems of learning opportunities that transcend institutions (e.g. 'credit bank system',[6] 'student-based funding',[7] 'lifelong learning passports').[8]
- Stronger components of generic education in higher learning (e.g. in engineering,[9] business,[10] and journalism).[11]
- Reforms towards generic undergraduate programmes (e.g. in Europe).[12]
- More room for diverse learning experiences. Reduction of the formal curriculum, reduction of public examination subjects, 'conceptual science'.[13]

- Various measures to mobilise community resource and facilities in order to provide diverse learning opportunities.[14]
- More opportunities for constructive, open-ended learning and group learning.
- More emphasis on tacit knowledge,[15] values education, civic education, character education, moral education and social competence.

Challenges ahead

The real challenge is yet to come. If the institutional control of knowledge is gradually fading away, what role will schools play in the new society? If transmission of information and factual knowledge is no longer the core function of schools, what *is* their core function? And indeed what is the function of teachers? If learning does not follow the industrial structure, what will the new format for learning at 'school age' be? If learning is a constructive process and learning outcomes have to be viewed in a postmodern perspective, how can we conceive successes and failures among students? If student learning runs across subjects, towards more group construction, more integration, greater application, what would all that imply for 'schools' as they are now?

Society has changed. It started with the economy, reinforced by technologies, but is now affecting all aspects of human lives. However, social institutions are yet to adapt themselves to the change. The notion of jobs, the notion of salaries, the notion of civil service and other similar assumptions, have all met unprecedented challenges. Education is no exception, and perhaps is one of the strongest institutions of the industrial society.[16]

My colleague Ian Hart gave a paper in Paris in 2001 revisiting Ivan Illich.[17] I am not an advocate of deschooling and it must be remembered that Illich developed his thesis in a totally different context. Nor will the institution of school collapse overnight. However, I am convinced that things do move very fast and that it will not be very long before the real challenge is felt. Most of the dramatic and fundamental challenges will surely emerge in our lifetime.

However, if we are educators in the best sense of that word, we have to put students' future to the forefront in all our considerations. And then we have to ask ourselves: Are we preparing our students for their future? The greatest challenge is perhaps not the change in our society, nor the educational reforms that arise as a consequence, but the assumptions in our minds about what education should be, what schools should be, how students should learn, and what teachers' role should be. It is time to rethink!

Notes

1 This was predicted by Peter Drucker in 1988. See P. Drucker (1988) Coming of the new organisation, collected in *Harvard Business Review on Knowledge Management*, pp. 1–19. Cambridge, MA: Harvard Business School Press.

2 Quoted from Senge, P. (2000) *Schools that Learn*, p. 42. New York: Doubleday.

3 'With the exception of Canada, France and Germany, participation in tertiary education has grown in all [OECD] countries between 1995 and 1999; in the majority of countries by more than 15% and in Hungary, Korea and Poland by between 40% and 84%.' Quoted from OECD (2001) *Education at a Glance*, p. 148. Paris: OECD.

4 Singapore has increased its higher education enrolment to 60 per cent (university and polytechnic) and is aiming at a higher rate; mainland China has since 1999 doubled its higher education enrolment and its total higher education students population is on a par with the USA; Taiwan eliminated its unified examination for higher education entrance in 2002, because there was an oversupply of places.

5 Started in MacMaster University some 20 years ago and now widespread in various parts of the world, initially in medical education, but extending to other kinds of studies.

6 This is a system introduced in South Korea in 1999. Students who have obtained 140 credit units from any accredited institution, even separately, are granted qualification by the state. See 'Credit unit bank in South Korea' (Chinese translation) (1999), in *Review of Foreign Higher Education Teaching and Research* (Beijing), 2(2).

7 This started in Australia in 1999, where government funding to graduate students is channelled directly to the students rather than through institutions. See Harman, G. (1999) 'Voucher and student-centred funding: the 1996–1998 Australian review of higher education financing and policy', *Higher Education Policy* 12(4): 219–35.

8 This is a notion that has aroused much discussion and has been endorsed in principle in Taiwan. Each citizen will be given a lifelong learning passport that will register the person's learning experiences in a cumulative way, and may be awarded qualifications accordingly independent of the institution.

9 The Washington Accord expects all engineering undergraduate programmes to have at least one-third of the curriculum in non-engineering studies.

10 The average undergraduate business curriculum in North America devotes 50 per cent of its programmes to non-business studies.

11 Typical undergraduate journalism programmes in North America comprise 70 per cent generic courses not directly related to journalism.

12 In the Bologna Declaration (1999) there was a general orientation to expect all European systems of higher education to reduce their undergraduate ('first cycle') duration to a minimum of three years of generic studies, and to leave specialisation to the 'second cycle'.

See http://www.unige.ch/cre/activities/Bologna%20Forum/Bologne1999/bologna%20declaration.htm.

In the UK, David Blunkett announced in February 2000 the introduction of a two-year generic Foundations Degree after A levels, such that specialisation takes place in the second degree. See http://www.dfee.gov.uk/speeches/15_02_00/index.shtml.

13 Moves in the USA, UK and China where unnecessary calculations and formulae are removed in physics and chemistry in order to give way to broader exposure and deeper understanding of science concepts.

14 A typical example is Viva Musica in Australia, where musicians organise themselves to provide first-rate musical experiences to schoolchildren.

15 See, for example, the relevant works by Robert Sternberg.

16 Readers may like to read more insightful discussions along these lines in Carnoy, M. (2000) *Sustaining the New Economy*. Cambridge, MA: Harvard University Press.

17 Hart, I. (2001) Deschooling and the Web: Ivan Illich 30 years on, *Education Media International*, 38(2/3): 69–76.

Conclusion
Reflections on democracy and school effectiveness

Lejf Moos and John MacBeath

Democracy. An idea to conjure with. It is a term with so many meanings, such different resonances in different contexts and cultures. Representatives of three Scandinavian countries (Lejf Moos, Jorunn Møller and Mats Ekholm) have addressed issues of democracy not only shaped by their respective cultural histories but by their particular responses to globalisation and the international movement of ideas. Assumptions of managerialism and performativity sit less easily in their context than in the USA or UK where hierarchy and the power of the principal or 'head' is a less contested notion. Denmark, Norway and Sweden share what we might, from the outside, perceive as a 'Scandinavian' perspective but, from the inside, cherish their distinctive identities as much as any other European country. They are a forceful reminder that context matters, and that to understand democratic learning is to grasp the nature of its intricate weave – politically, socially, economically and historically.

The approach to democracy from Karen Seashore Louis in the USA is more guarded. Democracy may have defeated various forms of totalitarianism but, she says, we are still entangled in competing visions of democracy, slogans and theories, attractive in isolation but problematic in practice. Democracy is a concept that is easy to embrace wholeheartedly but often too absent-mindedly. Her differentiation of liberal democracy (USA), social democracy (Sweden) and democracy as participation, is a helpful caveat. There is common ground here with the tensions identified by Labaree (discussed by John MacBeath) among three distinctive purposes of education – social choice, social promotion and democratic equality. These play out differently at different times in history and in different places. While in the USA and the UK, choice and social promotion have assumed a higher policy priority than democratic equality under the Reagan, Bush, Thatcher and Blair administrations, in the Scandinavian countries there is an unpredictability and volatility as the political colour of governments changes and responds to shifting global trends.

The influence of culture and history, the volatility of government, the struggle for democracy are all given a still sharper edge in the context of Third World countries. Democracy acquires its own meanings in the transition from paternalism to grass roots participation and, as Kathryn Riley suggests in her chapter, Guinea has perhaps something to teach us about bottom-up improvement.

The old established democracies struggle equally to resolve the tensions between political rhetoric and lived experience. Sweden, while consistently to the fore in discussions of democracy, is in an ambivalent period in its development. Mats Ekholm discusses findings from a small longitudinal study of students' perceptions of educational democracy and reaches a gloomy conclusion, echoed by personal testimony of students themselves in which the gap between words and deeds was unequivocally exposed. As Per Schulz Jørgensen suggests in his discussion of students' rights, we seriously underestimate their capacity for original and subversive thought. We cannot divorce (as schools often try to do) pupils' inner subjective construction of the world and their need to test out those models in the outer learning environment.

Yet, as so powerfully illustrated by Michael Schratz and Ulrike Löffler-Anzböck, children and young people exist in a school world which deprecates their experience, tolerating it only as long as it doesn't interfere with adult values. While young people live much of their lives in a rich visual environment and are often expert in that form of communication, they are required to learn in situations where the linear written and spoken word is the predominant register. It is the medium in which teachers are most comfortable and one in which they are most easily able to exert control. It is an exemplification of 'power over' as against 'power with', the latter a sharing of power which may be realised when pupils and teachers view their school experience through a different lens.

Young people feel a need to push at the boundaries of their schools and their societies. The more compliant and socially conservative their teachers, parents and leaders, the less young people themselves are likely to accept those strictures. They are less ready than their grandparents' generation to simply defer to institutional authority, to accord unconditional respect to elders. They are suspicious of them as 'betters'. They share more common frames of reference with youth in other countries than with adults in their own country. They demonstrate an affinity with a global designer culture tailor made for youth and impenetrable by their parents.

It is not only young people who embrace 'the universal product' as Hampden-Turner (1993) calls it. Politicians and policy makers also strive for uniformity and generality, argues Kathryn Riley, echoing Habermas. Their aspiration is for European or even global measures of quality and outcomes so that all countries can be benchmarked and administrators would be able to set still better, more competitive, normative targets. In this new market-driven age, politicians like to portray schools as small businesses, competing for clients. Headteachers are cast as efficient and effective managers of staff, finance and plant. In the now widely accepted vocabulary of the business world, teachers are required to 'deliver': to deliver on time, at key stages, to preset targets and to cost. And, of course, with value-added. Even in Norway, as Jorunn Møller tells us, politicians and chief executives assert that education policy can no longer be entrusted to teachers but should be driven by criteria established outside the profession.

Why can't school be more like the business world? ask politicians. Perhaps because the 'business world' is not some uniform body of practice. Kai-ming Cheng's analysis of a corporate world is far removed from the industrial model which schools have been exhorted to emulate. The businesses he describes are 'just-in-time', on-demand learning organisations; versatile, collaborative, with few layers or lines of command, vesting trust and decision-making powers in front-line people who present and represent the organisation. This is the model that he presents as a challenge to educational institutions, characterised, or caricatured perhaps, as hierarchical, bureaucratic, divisive and obsessed with boundaries – around subjects, outcomes, status, classrooms, timetables. His challenge to schools is to develop into knowledge-producing, rather than knowledge-consuming, communities. Knowledge in schools and in commercial organisations does, of course, have different objectives and underpinning values. Schools are, as is implicit in many of the chapters, committed to intellectual and moral subversion in an increasingly anti-intellectual and amoral society. Mats Ekholm's description of schools providing 'a vaccine against fascism' has interesting parallels with Hartman von Hentig's letter to Tobias, quoted in Chapter 1, which portrays schools as, above all, moral communities, bulwarks against extremism and undemocratic values. And, in the context of leadership, Alma Harris warns that while technical-rational approaches to leadership may be beguilingly attractive, they are unlikely to result in improved schooling unless accompanied by a moral dimension.

However, as Karen Seashore Louis points out, no liberal democracies have yet succeeded in establishing consensus around what the outcomes of schooling should be. There is, from generation to generation, an ebb and flow of educational priorities in response to economic and political change. Without a broad consensus on what education is *for*, that contested space is occupied by an implicit, and increasingly explicit, ideology of closing the gap, of raising standards among the trailing edge of low achievers because they are cast as a potential drain on the economy. So, with this as their guiding principle of education's intent, OECD, TIMSS, IEA and other comparative indicators are treated reverently and with angst by politicians. We are reminded, in Chapter 1, of the Berliner and Biddle (1995: 172) maxim:

- evidence attracts misinterpretation;
- misinterpretation attracts advocates and scoundrels;
- advocates and scoundrels attract the press and the multitudes who prefer to be told tales than to look at the evidence.

It is time to study the evidence. But time is what is currently in shortest supply. Time ticks differently in the political arena than in the classroom or in the mind of a child. Political lifetimes are short and politicians want quick fixes. Educators see learning as lifelong and schools work on a 10–15-year learning span.

For teachers there is little time to look at the evidence. Intensifying the teaching day, the teaching week, the teaching year may be seen by conspiracy theorists as a helpful political distraction. Keeping teachers busy prevents them from seeing the bigger picture or asking the subversive questions. But it is vital that they think and choose for themselves, and address future options with an informed understanding of where global forces are pushing them. The dilemma for teachers is between holding on and letting go. Teachers in twenty-first century schools will need to let go of a lot of their most cherished ways of doing things, but they will also have to be cautious in simply embracing mandated change. Schools need to hold on to what they have traditionally valued in education but with a discriminating eye, a clarity of focus and a commitment to changing what needs to be changed.

It is time to look more closely and with heightened critical understanding at the evidence from three decades of school effectiveness research and its translation into a policy, national and international. There is much to be learned from a closer focus on the outcomes and assumptions of that canon of work. Consistently through its findings we learn that the most significant determinants of achievement lie in home and community. What politicians have chosen to cherry-pick from the findings, however, is that schools make a difference, often with the invidious implication that schools make *all* the difference. Mats Ekholm's chronicling of effectiveness and improvement research around the world illustrates the significant contribution it has made to our understanding, but it has also constrained the debate. It has fuelled both external and internal (self) evaluation but also contributed to a narrowing of our measures of schooling and what school is for. It has sharpened our facility for measuring attainment outcomes but contributed little to our understanding of what democracy means in a school context.

Schools, in each of the societies represented, as Lejf Moos reminds us in the Introduction to the book, are places where cultural transmission and cultural transformation take place. They are not just about 'adding value' in basic skills or enhancement of test scores but are about *Bildung* – a word for which there is no English equivalent, but a term close to 'liberal education', a term that carries within it a notion of growing, filling out, becoming a whole person. School education has, for Michael Schratz and Ulrike Löffler-Anzböck, an emancipatory function and pupils, they show us, can play a role in reconstructing the social architecture of their classrooms and their schools.

As it has grown in sophistication, school effectiveness has turned its focus more sharply on the classroom and on teaching and learning. It has furthered our understanding of teaching but has still to get to grips seriously with the learning agenda. A continuous thread through these chapters is the shift from a teaching to a learning focus. This may seem by now platitudinous but it is radical in its implications. The notion of a learning-centred school is unnerving for management because it complicates managerial accountability. It is unsettling for teachers because it requires a paradigm shift in pedagogy, in school structures and in culture. It crosses the boundaries of classroom and home, school and community. It is lifelong and life-wide, continuous and permeating. It is underpinned by a conception of learning as a potentially more open, more accessible and more democratic process than at any other time in history. It blurs the roles of teachers and learners. It problematises knowledge acquisition and knowledge creation. In schools which have risen to the challenge, pupils have come to be seen as a rich untapped resource for knowledge creation.

More than at any time in history teachers are now willing to learn from their students, not only in obvious areas such as IT, where a 7-year-old can often be more skilled and knowledgeable than her teacher, but in respect of learning itself. With a proliferating literature on the brain, multiple intelligences and metacognition, teachers have become increasingly aware of how much they still have to learn and what a rich resource their pupils can be in making the learning journey together (MacBeath *et al.* 2002).

Kathryn Riley's conclusion from an in-depth study in the North of England is that schools are failing not because they need tighter structures, tougher targets, more discipline, stronger leadership, but because education has become a fragmented process. It is too joyless, too narrow, too externally driven and with too little scope for flexibility, risk and experimentation. Alma Harris' report from a study of schools in challenging circumstances shows that principals are concerned with vision and values, distributing leadership, being involved in staff development, relations and community building. To those school leaders, management is seen to be a short-term solution only.

Schools are likely to be better, more democratic, more professionally satisfying, more joyful places, concludes Jorunn Møller, when there is:

- an open flow of ideas regardless of their popularity;
- faith in the individual and collective capacity of people to create opportunities for solving problems;
- critical reflection, analysis and evaluation of ideas, problems and policies;
- concern for the welfare of others and the common good;
- concern for the dignity and rights of individuals and minorities;
- an understanding that democracy is less an ideal but something that needs to be *lived*;
- the organisation of social institutions so as to promote a democratic way of life.

All this requires a paradigm shift in notions of accountability from economic accountability to democratic accountability. For teachers, for school leaders and for those of us who work with them in partnership, it requires less subservience and a greater willingness to challenge orthodoxy and false gods. We need to reassert the democratic values that lie at the very heart of school education and move them into a wider public discourse. We need to educate the public, our political masters and, not least, ourselves.

References

Berliner, D.C. and Biddle, B.J. (1995) *The Manufactured Crisis: Myths, Fraud and Attack on America's Public Schools.* Reading, MA: Perseus Books.

Hampden-Turner, C. and Trompenaars, L. (1993) *The Seven Cultures of Capitalism.* New York: Doubleday.

MacBeath J. and Sugimine, H. with Sutherland, G. and Nishimura, M. (2002) *Self-evaluation in the Global Classroom.* London, Routledge.

Index

Page numbers in *italics* refer to figures and tables, *a* indicates appendix.

200   *Index*